# America's Str

# America's Strategic Posture

## The Final Report of the Congressional Commission on the Strategic Posture of the United States

William J. Perry, Chairman
James R. Schlesinger, Vice-Chairman

| | |
|---|---|
| Harry Cartland | Fred Ikle |
| John Foster | Keith Payne |
| John Glenn | Bruce Tarter |
| Morton Halperin | Ellen Williams |
| Lee Hamilton | James Woolsey |

UNITED STATES INSTITUTE OF PEACE PRESS
Washington, D.C.

United States Institute of Peace
1200 17th Street NW
Washington, DC 20036-3011
www.usip.org

First published 2009

Printed in the United States of America

The paper used in this publication meets the minimum requirements of American National Standards for Information Science—Permanence of Paper for Printed Library Materials, ANSI Z39.48-1984.

ISBN 978-1-60127-045-0

# Contents

# Letter from the Facilitating Organization

The initiative for a bipartisan, independent, forward-looking assessment of America's strategic posture came from the U.S. Congress in 2008. The United States Institute of Peace has been privileged to serve as the project facilitator while the Congressional Commission investigated, discussed, and crafted its final report. As a national institution established and funded by Congress, it is dedicated to playing an active part in the prevention, management, and resolution of threats to international peace. The Institute additionally helps to adapt the country's foreign policy and security practices to meet contemporary challenges. Its status as an independent, nonpartisan national organization ensures even-handed analysis and the ability to foster bipartisan action.

There is no greater global imperative than that of securing the nuclear peace of the world. Assessing the appropriate role for nuclear weapons, arms control initiatives, and nonproliferation programs are vital to defining America's strategic posture. This report comes at a time when threats have changed and the world has moved closer to a proliferation "tipping point." Armed conflicts, ethnic and religious strife, extremism, terrorism, and the proliferation of weapons of mass destruction all pose significant challenges to security and development worldwide. The spread of nuclear weapons and technologies adds a dangerous dimension to that global environment. Implementation of this final report's recommendations will demand a tremendous amount of political will and cooperation by the Executive and Legislative branches of our government, and require public education and support for the policies. It is my hope that the United States Institute of Peace will continue to provide a forum for expert discussion and a platform for public education on these issues.

I am deeply grateful to former Secretaries of Defense William S. Perry and James R. Schlesinger for their leadership of this Congressional Commission on the Strategic Posture of the United States and to all the commissioners for their hard work and dedication to this project: former senator John Glenn, Dr. John Foster, former congressman Lee Hamilton, ambassador Jim Woolsey, Dr. Mort Halperin, Dr. Keith Payne, Dr. Ellen Williams, Dr. Harry Cartland, Dr. Bruce Tarter, and Dr. Fred Ikle.

I also want to thank the staff who worked on the project, and all the experts who contributed knowledge of national security, arms control, nuclear technology, and military affairs. In particular, I want to acknowledge the work of Paul Hughes, the Commission's executive director and senior program officer in the Center for Conflict Analyses and Prevention at the Institute. I also want to thank the Institute for Defense Analyses for its excellent support of this endeavor.

Reaching agreement on the strategic posture of the United States is no easy task. It will now fall to the President, Congress, and the American people to demonstrate the wisdom and judgment to carry out the recommendations and ideas expressed in this report. I have no doubt they will meet the challenge.

Sincerely,

Richard H. Solomon, *President*
*United States Institute of Peace*

# Chairman's Preface

Last year the Congress authorized the formation of a commission to conduct a review of the strategic posture of the United States and to make recommendations on how to move forward. Congress then appointed a 12-person bipartisan group to conduct this review, and asked me to be Chairman and Jim Schlesinger to be Vice-Chairman. This Commission has deliberated for the last eleven months and is now prepared to report to the administration, to the Congress, and to the American people. Our observations, findings, and recommendations follow. This preface offers some personal observations to frame and help summarize our work. The Commission agreed that, as long as other nations have nuclear weapons, the United States must continue to safeguard its security by maintaining an appropriately effective nuclear deterrent force. Safeguarding U.S. security also requires that the United States should continue to lead international efforts to prevent the proliferation of nuclear weapons, reduce the number of nuclear weapons worldwide, and provide better protection for the residual nuclear forces and fissile material.

This basic strategy has deep foundations in U.S. policy; nevertheless we recognize that it will be difficult to execute. It will require a thoughtful analysis of the new security problems we face today in order to arrive at the right policy balance between these two different ways of safeguarding our security. It will require U.S. leadership abroad, with an emphasis on leadership by example. And it will require bipartisan consensus at home on these transcendentally important nuclear issues. The American nuclear posture has been, and will continue to be, highly controversial, including among commission members. Nevertheless our commission was able to reach consensus language on most of the critical issues related to military capabilities, nonproliferation initiatives, and arms control strategies of the United States. Commission members came from a broad spectrum of the American political scene, and, not surprisingly, faced major challenges in trying to reach consensus. Despite our differences, we were able to find consensus on all but one significant policy issue. We hope that the Executive Branch and the Congress will also face these critical policy issues with a bipartisan spirit.

I believe that this is a moment of opportunity but also urgency. The opportunity arises from the arrival of the new administration in Washington and the top-down reassessment that must now begin of national security strategy and of the purposes of U.S. nuclear weapons. The opportunity also arises because the Russian government has indicated a readiness to undertake a serious dialogue with the United States on strategic issues. The urgency arises from the imminent danger of nuclear terrorism if we pass a tipping point in nuclear proliferation, and because of an accumulation of difficult decisions affecting our nuclear posture.

Nuclear weapons have safeguarded our security for decades during the Cold War by deterring an attack on the United States or its allies. We will need to maintain this deterrence capability for some years to come. On the other hand, if nuclear weapons were to fall into the hands of a terror organization, they could pose an extremely serious threat to our security, and one for which deterrence would not be applicable. This is not a theoretical danger. Al Qaeda, for example, has declared that obtaining a nuclear weapon is a "holy duty" for its members. Fortunately, no terror group is able to build a nuclear weapon from scratch, but as new nations achieve a nuclear weapons capability, the probability increases that one of these new nuclear powers will either sell or lose control of its fissile material or even one of its bombs. This is also not a theoretical danger, as illustrated by A. Q. Khan's black market in nuclear materials and technology. Thus, preventing nuclear terrorism is closely tied to preventing the proliferation of nuclear weapons. But we are in danger of losing the battle to stop proliferation. Under the guise of a nuclear power program, North Korea has developed a small nuclear arsenal in the last few years. Iran appears to be following in its footsteps, and other nations, particularly in the Mideast, are starting nuclear power programs using Iran as a model. Thus, the proliferation of nuclear weapons and fissile materials is dangerously close to a "tipping point."

While the programs that maintain our deterrence force are primarily national, the programs that prevent proliferation and safeguard nuclear weapons and fissile material are primarily international. Indeed, it is clear that we cannot meet our goal of reducing the proliferation threat without substantial international cooperation, for example in bringing effective global economic pressure on Iran and North Korea. But cooperation of other nations increasingly depends on whether these nations perceive that the U.S. and Russia are moving to seriously reduce the salience of nuclear weapons in their own force posture and are continuing to make significant reductions in their nuclear arsenal. This has been called into question with the new nuclear programs and rhetoric in Russia, the debate in the U.S. about nuclear weapons being used for tactical roles (nuclear bunker busters) and by a perceived stall in formal arms control treaties. Thus U.S. nuclear forces must be postured to have the needed deterrence benefits but also to promote the international cooperation needed for preventing and rolling back proliferation. In any complex strategy involving multiple goals and policies a balance must be struck that promotes complementary effects. But sometimes there are tradeoffs and these must be faced squarely. It is possible that the different policies to achieve these different security requirements will be in conflict. In fact much of the disagreement in our commission arose because some commissioners give a priority to dealing with one security need while others give a priority to dealing with the other. But throughout the deliberations of the commission, all of our members sought to strike a balance that supports to reasonable levels both of these security needs. To a large extent, we were able to meet that goal.

The need to strike such a balance has been with us at least since the ending of the Cold War. President Clinton's nuclear posture spoke of the need to "lead but hedge." That policy called for the United States to lead the world in nuclear arms reductions and in programs to prevent the proliferation of nuclear weapons, while at the same time maintaining a nuclear deterrent force that hedged against adverse geopolitical developments. The leadership aspect of this policy was demonstrated most vividly by a cooperative program with Russia, established under the bipartisan Nunn-Lugar Program, which was responsible for the dismantlement of more than 4,000 nuclear weapons and assisted Ukraine, Belarus, and Kazakhstan in removing all of their nuclear weapons. U.S. leadership was also demonstrated by signing the Comprehensive Test Ban Treaty (CTBT) and negotiating with Russia a new arms control treaty, neither of which, however, was ratified by the Senate. The Bush administration initially took a different view of overall strategic priorities, but last year Secretary Gates explicitly reaffirmed that the American nuclear posture would be based on "lead but hedge."

President Obama has stated that the United States should work towards the goal of the global elimination of nuclear weapons. But he has also said that until that goal is reached, he is committed to maintain a nuclear deterrent that is safe, secure, and reliable. This is, in a sense, the most recent formulation of the "lead but hedge" policy. All of the commission members believe that reaching the ultimate goal of global nuclear elimination would require a fundamental change in geopolitics. Indeed, if the vision of nuclear elimination is thought of as the "top of the mountain," it is clear that it cannot be seen at this time. But I believe that we should be heading up the mountain to a "base camp" that would be safer than where we are today. And I also believe that getting the international political support necessary to move to this base camp will be greatly facilitated if the United States is seen as working for the ultimate elimination of nuclear weapons. At the base camp, we would have nuclear forces that are safe, secure and can reliably serve the perceived need for deterrence and extended deterrence; we would be headed in the direction of nuclear elimination; and our nuclear forces would be stable—that is, they should be sustainable even under normal fluctuations in geopolitical conditions. This base camp concept serves as an organizing principle for my own thinking about our strategic posture, since it allows the United States to both lead and hedge. While some of the commissioners do not accept the feasibility or even the desirability of seeking global elimination, all commissioners accept the view that the United States must support programs that both lead and hedge. That is, all commissioners support programs that move in two parallel paths—one path which reduces nuclear dangers by maintaining our deterrence, and the other which reduces nuclear dangers through arms control and international programs to prevent proliferation.

The first path—reducing nuclear dangers through deterrence—includes clarifying our declaratory policy by stating that our nuclear forces are intended for deterrence of an attack against the United States or its allies, and would be used only as a defensive last resort. This policy would by backed up with programs that assure that our nuclear forces are safe, secure, and reliable, and in sufficient quantities to perform their deterrent tasks. Our report spells out a number of steps needed to maintain the effectiveness of the stockpile as long as it is needed. Foremost among these is providing robust support for the technical programs at the weapon laboratories, including continuing to push the frontiers of computing and simulation and enhancing the laboratories' experimental capabilities. The weapons labs have achieved remarkable success with the Stockpile Stewardship Program and the Life Extension Program, but this will become more difficult as the weapons age. Moreover, continued success is endangered by recent personnel and funding cuts. We believe that the technical staff of the weapons labs is a unique national asset, and that this should be recognized by giving the labs an expanded national security role, to include fundamental research, energy technologies, and intelligence support. We recommend ways of enabling that expanded role. Besides dealing with the intellectual infrastructure of the weapons complex, we also make recommendations on how to sustain the aging physical infrastructure.

The second path—reducing nuclear dangers by arms control and preventing proliferation—includes negotiating arms reduction treaties with Russia that make significant reductions in the nuclear stockpiles of Russia and the United States, beginning with a follow-on treaty to replace the Strategic Arms Reduction Treaty (START) before it expires at the end of this year. We note that follow-on treaties entailing deeper reductions would require finding a way of dealing with very difficult problems, to include "tactical" nuclear forces, reserve weapons and bringing in other nuclear powers. We also recommend seeking a strategic dialogue with Russia broader than nuclear treaties, to include civilian nuclear energy, ballistic missile defenses, space systems, and ways of improving warning systems and increasing decision time. Although the dialogue with Russia is most important in the nuclear field, we also recommend renewing strategic dialogue with a broad set of states interested in strategic stability, including not just Russia and NATO allies but also China and U.S. allies and friends in Asia. Diplomatic efforts to prevent nuclear proliferation by Iran and to reverse proliferation by North Korea should also be reenergized. Commissioners also recommend that we seek global cooperation to deal with other potential proliferation concerns arising from the anticipated global expansion of civilian nuclear power. We agree that the United States should seek an international Fissile Material Cutoff Treaty, and prepare carefully for the NPT review conference in 2010. However, we have been unable to reach agreement on the ratification of the CTBT. My own view is that ratification of the CTBT would substantially enhance U.S. security and is an essential step in putting the United States in a leadership position in dealing with proliferation problems. However, the commission is divided on this issue, with some of the commissioners believing that ratification could endanger our security. In our report, we spell out the reasons behind these two conflicting points of view while also making some recommendations for the ratification review.

The commissioners know what direction they want to see the world headed. We reject the vision of a world defined over the next decade or two by a collapse of the nonproliferation regime, a cascade of proliferation to new states, an associated dramatic rise in the risks of nuclear terrorism, and a renewal of competition for nuclear advantage among the major powers. As pragmatic experts, we embrace a different vision. We see a world in which the occasional nonproliferation failure is counter-balanced by the occasional rollback of some and the continued restraint by the many. We see a world in which the risks of nuclear terrorism are steadily reduced through stronger cooperative measures to control their access to materials, technology, and expertise. And we see a world of cooperation among the major powers that ensures strategic stability and order, and steadily diminishes reliance on nuclear weapons to preserve world peace. We believe that implementation of the strategy we recommend will help the United States lead the global effort to bring this world into being.

# Executive Summary

U.S. nuclear strategy begins with the central dilemma that nuclear weapons are both the greatest potential threat to our way of life and important guarantors of U.S. security. A breakdown of international nuclear order would be a catastrophe for the United States among many others. Preservation of that order requires that we work to reduce nuclear dangers by effective deterrence, arms control, and nonproliferation.

This is a moment of opportunity to revise and renew U.S. nuclear strategy, but also a moment of urgency. The opportunity arises from the arrival of a new administration in Washington and the top-down reassessment that must now begin of national security strategy, of approaches to nuclear security, and of the purposes of U.S. nuclear weapons and their supporting capabilities. The urgency follows, internationally, from the danger that we may be close to a tipping point in nuclear proliferation and, domestically, from an accumulation of delayed decisions about the nuclear weapon program.

*This is a moment of opportunity to revise and renew U.S. nuclear strategy, but also a moment of urgency....The urgency follows, internationally, from the danger that we may be close to a tipping point in nuclear proliferation and, domestically, from an accumulation of delayed decisions about the nuclear weapon program.*

In addressing the challenges of nuclear security for the decades ahead, the United States must pursue a comprehensive strategy. So long as nuclear dangers remain, it must have a strong deterrent that is effective in meeting its security needs and those of its allies. This is a challenge that has changed fundamentally over the last two decades—and largely for the better. The nuclear deterrent of the United States need not play anything like the central role that it did for decades in U.S. military policy and national security strategy. But it remains crucial for some important problems.

While deterrence plays an essential role in reducing nuclear dangers, it is not the only means for doing so, and accordingly the United States must seek additional cooperative measures of a political kind, including for example arms control and nonproliferation. This is a time when these approaches can be renewed and reenergized.

These components of strategy must be integrated into a comprehensive approach. They can be mutually complementary and self-reinforcing. But sometimes there are conflicts and trade-offs, and these must be clearly identified and hard choices made.

The body of this report includes a total of nearly 100 findings and recommendations. These elaborate constructive steps that can be taken now to adapt the components of strategy to the challenges and opportunities in front of the nation. The main themes of these findings and recommendations are as follows.

**On the security environment:** Over the last two decades, the security environment of the United States has changed considerably and generally for the better. The threat of nuclear Armageddon has largely receded. At the height of the Cold War, the U.S. nuclear arsenal numbered over 32,000 weapons and the Soviet arsenal over 45,000; today, the United States has reduced its arsenal of operationally deployed strategic nuclear warheads to approximately 2,000 and Russia is not far behind. The two have also withdrawn about 14,000 tactical nuclear weapons from forward deployments. But new challenges have emerged, especially the threat of nuclear terrorism and increased proliferation. The opportunities to further engage Russia and China, as well as U.S. allies and other partners, to meet these new challenges are rising. President Obama has pledged to work for the global elimination of nuclear weapons, but until that happens, to maintain a safe, secure, and reliable deterrent force. The conditions that might make possible the global elimination of nuclear weapons are not present today and their creation would require a fundamental transformation of the world political order. But this report spells out many steps that can significantly reduce nuclear dangers and that are available now.

> *The nuclear force of the United States is a small fraction of what it was at the end of the Cold War and the U.S. reliance on nuclear weapons in national military strategy and national security strategy has been reduced.*

**On the U.S. nuclear posture:** The principal functions of the U.S. nuclear posture are to create the conditions in which nuclear weapons are never used, to assure allies of the U.S. commitment to their security, and to discourage unwelcome competition while encouraging strategic cooperation. Though the Cold War calculus to achieve these goals was effective at the time, the U.S. nuclear posture needs to change to cope with the new, more complex and fluid threat environment. A great deal of change has already occurred. The nuclear force of the United States is a small fraction of what it was at the end of the Cold War and the U.S. reliance on nuclear weapons in national military strategy and national security strategy has been substantially reduced. This process can continue, assuming that Russia is willing to remain involved in the process. The sizing of U.S. forces remains overwhelmingly driven by the requirements of essential equivalence and strategic stability with Russia. For the deterrence of attacks by regional aggressors and even China, the force structure requirements are relatively modest. The focus on Russia is not because the United States and Russia are enemies; they are not. No one seriously contemplates a direct Russian attack on the United States. Some U.S. allies located closer to Russia, however, are fearful of Russia and its tactical nuclear forces. The imbalance in non-strategic nuclear weapons, which greatly favors Russia, is of rising concern and an illustration of the new challenges of strategic stability as reductions in strategic weapons proceed. The need to reassure U.S. allies and also to hedge against a possible turn for the worse in Russia (or China)

> *The United States should underscore that it conceives of and prepares for the use of nuclear weapons only for the protection of itself and its allies in extreme circumstances.*

points to the fact that the U.S. nuclear posture must be designed to address a very broad set of U.S. objectives, including not just deterrence of enemies in time of crisis and war but also assurance of our allies and dissuasion of potential adversaries. Indeed, the assurance function of the force is as important as ever. The triad of strategic nuclear delivery systems should be maintained for the immediate future and this will require some difficult investment choices. The same is true for delivery systems of non-strategic nuclear weapons.

**On missile defense:** Missile defenses can play a useful role in supporting the basic objectives of deterrence, broadly defined. Defenses that are effective against regional aggressors are a valuable component of the U.S. strategic posture. The United States should develop and, where appropriate, deploy missile defenses against regional nuclear aggressors, including against limited long-range threats. These can also be beneficial for limiting damage if deterrence fails. The United States should ensure that its actions do not lead Russia or China to take actions that increase the threat to the United States and its allies and friends.

**On declaratory policy:** Declaratory policy is a signal of U.S. intent to both friends and prospective enemies and thus an important aspect of the overall strategic posture. To be effective, it must be understood to reflect the intentions of national leadership. While an element of calculated ambiguity remains essential, there should be enough clarity that potential foes will be deterred. The United States should underscore that it conceives of and prepares for the use of nuclear weapons only for the protection of itself and its allies in extreme circumstances.

**On the nuclear weapons stockpile:** So long as it continues to rely on nuclear deterrence, the United States requires a stockpile of nuclear weapons that are safe, secure, and reliable, and whose threatened use in military conflict would be credible. The Stockpile Stewardship Program and the Life Extension Program have been remarkably successful in refurbishing and modernizing the stockpile to meet these criteria, but cannot be counted on for the indefinite future. The Commission observes that the debate over the proposed Reliable Replacement Warhead revealed a lot of confusion about what was intended, what is needed, and what constitutes "new" and believes that, as the nation moves forward, it must be clear about what is being initiated (and what is not) as well as what makes a weapon "new" and what does not. Alternatives to stockpile stewardship and life extension involve to varying degrees the reuse and/or redesign of components and different engineering solutions. The decision on which approach is best should be made on a type-by-type basis as they age. So long as modernization proceeds within the framework of existing U.S. policy, it should encounter minimum political difficulty. As a matter of U.S. policy, the United States does not produce fissile materials and does not conduct nuclear explosive tests. Also the United States does not currently seek new weapons with new military characteristics. Within this framework, it should seek the possible benefits of improved safety, security, and reliability available to it.

**On the nuclear weapons complex:** The physical infrastructure is in serious need of transformation. The National Nuclear Security Administration (NNSA) has a reasonable plan but it lacks the needed funding. The intellectual infrastructure is also in trouble. Redesignating the weapons laboratories as national security laboratories and strengthening their cooperation with the Departments of Defense, State, and Homeland Security and also the intelligence community can help with both of these problems. NNSA has not achieved the original intent of the law that created it; it lacks the needed autonomy. This requires that the NNSA Act be amended to establish NNSA as a separate agency reporting to the President through the Secretary of Energy, along with other provisions aimed at ensuring the needed autonomy.

**On arms control:** The moment appears ripe for a renewal of arms control with Russia, and this bodes well for a continued reduction in the nuclear arsenal. The United States and Russia should pursue a step-by-step approach and take a modest first step to ensure that there is a successor to START I when it expires at the end of 2009. Beyond a modest incremental reduction in operationally deployed strategic nuclear weapons, the arms control process becomes much more complex as new factors are introduced. One of the most important factors will be the imbalance of non-strategic nuclear weapons. In support of its arms control interests and interest in strategic stability more generally, the

> *The moment appears ripe for a renewal of arms control with Russia, and this bodes well for a continued reduction in the nuclear arsenal.*

United States should pursue a much broader and more ambitious set of strategic dialogues with not just Russia but also China and U.S. allies in both Europe and Asia.

**On nonproliferation:** This is also an opportune moment to reenergize nonproliferation. Success in advancing U.S. nonproliferation interests requires U.S. leadership. Despite the occasional failure of nonproliferation, the historical track record is good, and there is good reason to hope for continued success in the years ahead. The risks of a proliferation "tipping point" and of nuclear terrorism underscore the urgency of acting now. The United States should pursue a broad agenda to strengthen the international treaty system and the institutions that support its effective functioning. It is especially important that it prepare to play a leadership role at the 2010 NPT Review Conference.

*This is also an opportune moment to reenergize nonproliferation. Success in advancing U.S. nonproliferation interests requires U.S. leadership.*

**On the Comprehensive Test Ban Treaty (CTBT):** The Commission has no agreed position on whether ratification of the CTBT should proceed. But recognizing that the President has called for the Senate to reconsider U.S. ratification, the Commission recommends a number of steps to enable Senate deliberation, including preparation of a comprehensive net assessment of benefits, costs, and risks that updates arguments from a decade ago.

**On prevention and protection:** Since nonproliferation does not always succeed and deterrence is sometimes unreliable, the overall strategy must be supplemented with additional steps to prevent nuclear proliferation and terrorism and protect ourselves from its consequences. The Commission supports measures such as the Proliferation Security Initiative and the Global Initiative to Combat Nuclear Terrorism and also encourages stronger "whole of government" approaches to reduce the risks of nuclear smuggling into the United States. We note also that the United States has done little to reduce its vulnerability to attack with electromagnetic pulse weapons and recommend that current investments in modernizing the national power grid take account of this risk.

**On visions of the future:** The Congress charged the Commission to look to the long term in formulating its recommendations about the U.S. strategic posture. As we have debated our findings and recommendations, it has become clear that we have very different visions of what might be possible in the long term. Fundamentally, this reflects our differences over whether the conditions can ever be created that might enable the elimination of nuclear weapons. But our debates have also brought home to us that, despite our differences over the long term, we share to a very significant degree a vision of the nearer term. And it is a hopeful vision. We reject the notion that somehow it is inevitable that international nuclear order will collapse. On the contrary—the past successes of the United States and its international partners in meeting and reducing nuclear dangers make us more hopeful for the future. We embrace the possibility that over the next decade or two nuclear dangers will be further reduced. Despite our many differences of opinion about possibilities and priorities, we have come together around a strategy that offers pragmatic steps for bringing this vision closer to reality. It is firmly grounded in the strategic tradition of the United States in balancing deterrence and other means, including principally arms control and nonproliferation, to reduce nuclear dangers. This strategy is also essential to the preservation of the tradition of nuclear non-use, which is now deeply rooted in six decades of experience and strongly serves U.S. interests.

> *[W]e have come together around a strategy that offers pragmatic steps.... It is firmly grounded in the strategic tradition of the United States in balancing deterrence and other means, including principally arms control and nonproliferation, to reduce nuclear dangers.*

# Introduction

The Congressional Commission on the Strategic Posture of the United States was chartered by the Congress to "examine and make recommendations with respect to the long-term strategic posture of the United States." The legislation defined the posture broadly, to include not just the nation's nuclear deterrent. It also asked that the Commission look broadly at the elements of national strategy, including both military and political instruments. The Commission was charged with drawing conclusions, developing findings, and making recommendations. This final report builds upon and extends our interim report of December 2008. We are grateful for this opportunity to serve the nation and look forward to continued engagement on these issues.

The Commission organized its work to address the following specific questions:

- What factors in the external security environment should inform U.S. policy and strategy?
- How has U.S. nuclear and strategic policy evolved since the end of the Cold War?
- What role should nuclear weapons and U.S. strategic military capabilities more generally (including missile defense) play today in U.S. military strategy and national security strategy?
- How should U.S. forces be postured? How many nuclear weapons are "enough?"
- How can political instruments be used to shape the security environment? What can arms control contribute? How can nonproliferation be strengthened?
- What is the most efficient and effective way to maintain a safe, secure, and reliable deterrent?

This final report documents the consensus reached by the Commission. Individual commissioners have expressed their support for its general conclusions and specific findings and recommendations, except in a few instances where specific dissents are noted. But the Commission has not sought to secure full agreement on the precise wording of each argument and every point and thus the views of individual commissioners may not fully align with each and every part of the report.

The report proceeds as follows. It begins with a review of the security environment. Chapter 1 describes how that environment has evolved over recent decades and highlights the key factors in the current environment that should inform U.S. policy and strategy. A key argument developed here is that this environment has evolved in distinct phases, each with its own set of challenges and opportunities. U.S. policy and strategy must be tailored to the specific challenges and opportunities of the current period. A balanced approach is needed, one that integrates military and political instruments of national power in a comprehensive approach to meet and reduce nuclear dangers.

The remainder of the report elaborates how this should be accomplished in the years ahead. Chapters 2 through 6 address different aspects of the U.S. strategic posture, including the nuclear force structure, missile defense, declaratory policy, the stockpile of nuclear weapons, and the weapons complex. Chapters 7 through 9 address different aspects of the political strategy supporting U.S. national objectives, including arms control and nonproliferation. This section includes a separate discussion of the Comprehensive Test Ban Treaty. Chapter 10 addresses additional preventive and protection measures. The report closes with some observations about the nature of the consensus achieved by the Commission. Appendices provide supplemental information about the work of the Commission.

# 1

# On Challenges and Opportunities

The formulation of policy and strategy should begin with a sound assessment of the international security environment. That assessment must clearly identify the specific dangers posed by nuclear weapons, both to the security of the United States and its allies and to international security more broadly. It must be specific about the policy challenges associated with those dangers. Such an assessment must also clearly identify the specific opportunities to reduce those dangers. As should be expected, these challenges and opportunities evolve over time, as international circumstances change. A brief historical review helps to bring home how much the international security environment has evolved over recent decades, and with it U.S. policy and strategy. It also helps to bring home some important elements of continuity in both the security environment and U.S. policy and strategy.

## The Cold War

In the immediate aftermath of the U.S. use of nuclear weapons to defeat an enemy that had caused very great numbers of casualties in World War II, there seemed to be a brief opportunity to avert nuclear competition and to create an international control regime for nuclear weapons. But this proved elusive as the Soviet Union grew increasingly intent on gaining geopolitical advantage in Europe and elsewhere in the late 1940s. Thereafter, the challenges for U.S. nuclear policy seemed many and the opportunities few.

The principal nuclear challenge throughout the Cold War was to ensure that deterrence functioned effectively. For decades, the United States and its allies faced a threat to their very existence from the Soviet Union and the Warsaw Pact. Throughout this period, Soviet and Warsaw Pact advantages in conventional military forces in Europe were seen as overwhelming. These were eventually reinforced by Soviet production of a massive nuclear arsenal and its efforts to gain a position of strategic superiority over the West. Accordingly, the United States fashioned a nuclear deterrent essentially to help keep the Cold War from going hot. The United States built a nuclear force designed primarily to deter an attack by the Soviet Union and its Warsaw Pact allies on Western Europe. Doing so helped make U.S. allies more secure and it also helped to counter the pressures on them to acquire nuclear weapons of their own. To ensure that its threats to use nuclear weapons were seen as credible in Moscow, the United States also had to focus on deterring attacks on U.S. nuclear forces stationed in the United States.

Maintenance of the U.S. nuclear deterrent required technologically ambitious national programs to ensure military operational effectiveness. The perceived needs of deterrence led to the development of a large and diverse arsenal. At its height in 1967, the U.S. arsenal of nuclear weapons numbered about 32,000 and included warheads for strategic missiles, tactical air-dropped bombs, nuclear artillery shells, nuclear land mines, nuclear torpedoes, and nuclear anti-ballistic missile warheads. The Soviet arsenal ultimately numbered over 45,000. Other countries, in particular France, the United Kingdom, and China, developed nuclear weapons as well, but in far smaller numbers—the low hundreds.

A key challenge of this period was to maintain strategic stability even as the two sides modernized their strategic arsenals and as the Soviets strived for advantage. The United States sought to constrain the nuclear competition while also managing it in a way that would limit its costs and risks. Arms control played a role in this period in limiting the arms build up (under the Strategic Arms Limitation Treaty).

The primary opportunity of the Cold War period was to create a nonproliferation regime. In the 1950s and 1960s, many states faced choices about pursuing national nuclear weapons programs and capabilities of their own and chose not to do so. Many states also sought the benefits of the peaceful uses of nuclear science, including primarily for energy production. But they were also concerned about the illicit diversion of nuclear science from legitimate, civilian activity to military purposes, and from states to non-state actors, including criminals and terrorists. Accordingly, it was possible in this period to construct a nonproliferation regime. This was done in phases, first in the 1950s with the establishment of the International Atomic Energy Agency to promote but also police the civilian use of nuclear science and then late in the 1960s with the negotiation of the Nuclear Non-Proliferation Treaty (NPT). The NPT recognized five states as nuclear-weapon states by virtue of their successful tests of nuclear devices prior to negotiation of the treaty (the United States, Soviet Union, Britain, France, and China) and they made a commitment under Article VI to work to end the arms race and ultimately relinquish their nuclear weapons in the context of general and complete global disarmament. These states are also the five permanent members of the United Nations Security Council (hereinafter referred to as the P-5).

This short review of Cold War history brings home a key point: from its earliest foundations, U.S. nuclear strategy has been guided by two key imperatives. The first is to reduce nuclear dangers with a deterrent that is strong and effective. The second is to utilize arms control and nonproliferation to further reduce those dangers. These objectives are self-reinforcing and the steps to achieve them should be complementary to the extent possible.

## From 1989 to 2009

The collapse of communist governments in Central and Eastern Europe and the demise of the Soviet Union had profound implications for U.S. nuclear policy and strategy. The challenges became less demanding, and the opportunities relatively more significant. At the same time, some new challenges emerged.

The challenge of deterring Soviet and Warsaw Pact conventional attack obviously disappeared. Dramatic steps were taken both bilaterally and unilaterally to stand down from nuclear confrontation, end the arms race, and reduce common nuclear dangers. Significant reductions in strategic nuclear forces were agreed in 1991, under the auspices of the Strategic Arms Reductions Treaty (START I), and in 2002, under the auspices of the Strategic Offensive Reduction Treaty (SORT), also known as the Treaty of Moscow. SORT commits the United States and Russia to reduce the number of their operationally deployed strategic nuclear warheads to between 2,200 and 1,700 by the end of 2012. In fact, the United States reduced its forces below the upper limit in late 2008. This is the lowest number of weapons deployed by the United States since the Eisenhower administration.

> *[F]rom its earliest foundations, U.S. nuclear strategy has been guided by two key imperatives. The first is to reduce nuclear dangers with a deterrent that is strong and effective. The second is to utilize arms control and nonproliferation to further reduce those dangers.*

The end of the Cold War also brought significant reductions of non-strategic nuclear capabilities. Approximately 14,000 tactical nuclear warheads were withdrawn from forward deployments by the United States and Russia under the Presidential Nuclear Initiatives (PNI) agreed by Presidents George H.W. Bush and Mikhail Gorbachev in 1991 and Boris Yeltsin in 1992. The United States withdrew nuclear artillery shells and warheads for short-range ballistic missiles and also all nuclear warheads from naval surface ships, attack submarines, and land-based naval aviation. These initiatives were politically binding commitments but also reciprocal in nature. Russia also promised to withdraw capabilities and to consolidate remaining non-strategic nuclear warheads at a smaller number of storage sites. These initiatives included steps to take some of the standing strategic forces off alert and to curtail various modernization programs.

The end of the Cold War also brought important questions about the fate of nuclear weapons and associated capabilities in states formerly a part of the Soviet Union but now independent—Ukraine, Kazakhstan, and Belarus. Through a carefully orchestrated process of political inducements, security assurances, and other measures, these states gave up their nuclear weapons capabilities.

The end of the Cold War also opened an opportunity to expand cooperation between Washington and Moscow to address the challenges of safety and security in the nuclear complex of the former Soviet Union. This so-called "loose nukes" problem has required extensive U.S. resources under the Cooperative Threat Reduction Program to safeguard weapons, materials, and facilities in Russia and elsewhere. This program has been a significant success.

In more general terms, the United States also faced a continuing challenge through this period of moving away from nuclear deterrence as the foundation of its relationship with Russia and achieving a fundamental shift in security relations. This effort has been complicated by continued uncertainty about whether Russia can or will become a stronger partner of the West in addressing common international security problems. It is further complicated by a difference of views about whether formal arms control measures help accomplish the political objective of deeper partnership or are so cumbersome and adversarial in character as to prove counterproductive. Accordingly, the emphasis in U.S. policy has shifted increasingly from deterrence to dissuasion, which is to say from a focus on preventing war and nuclear use to discouraging a Russian effort to renew nuclear competition in the quest for political advantage. But so long as each side must account for the fact that the other retains an operational capability that can destroy it, deterrence continues to play some role in the bilateral relationship, albeit one distinctly different from that of the Cold War.

*[The current level is] the lowest number of weapons deployed by the United States since the Eisenhower administration.*

This period also brought another important opportunity: to strengthen the nonproliferation regime. The effort to strengthen the regime was seen as especially urgent following revelations about illicit nuclear weapons activities in Iraq and North Korea. The opportunity to do so was underscored by the continuing convergence of the views of the major powers that they should play a leading role in doing so. The willingness of China and France to join the NPT in 1992 was noteworthy. At the NPT review conference of 1995, states parties were required to make a decision about the future of the treaty—about whether to extend it and if so for how long and under what conditions. A decision was taken to extend it indefinitely, in the context of a commitment to renew efforts by states parties to implement it more effectively. The United States played a leading role in the process leading to this decision.

In the period since the end of the Cold War, three significant challenges have emerged. Two were challenges throughout the Cold War but have gained new prominence over the last two decades: nuclear proliferation and nuclear terrorism. The third challenge is the newly unpredictable nature of the strategic environment.

During the Cold War, proliferation was strongly inhibited by the relationships of extended deterrence established by the United States (and also by the Soviet Union) and by creation of the nonproliferation regime. As noted above, there were even instances of successful proliferation "roll back" during the Cold War, including that of South Africa among others. But since the end of the Cold War, proliferation has also continued, as demonstrated by Iraq's nuclear weapons program and by nuclear tests by India and Pakistan in 1998 and North Korea in 2006. Today, Iran stands at the brink of nuclear weapons capability. Such proliferation is troubling for various reasons. It calls into question, in the minds of some, the viability of the nonproliferation regime. It stimulates interest in further proliferation among neighboring states. It raises questions about the safety and security of the nuclear arsenals and weapons establishments in these countries. It creates new supplier networks outside of existing international control mechanisms. Proliferation to belligerent states opposed to the United States and/or the regional status quo is particularly troubling for various reasons. It could lead some leaders to believe that they are able to use nuclear threats to coerce their neighbors or to deter the United States and/or international coalitions from protecting those neighbors. This could embolden belligerent states to commit acts of aggression or domestic transgressions that would require very risky efforts to redress. Such proliferation also increases the risk that nuclear weapons will end up in the hands of a terror group.

> *During the Cold War, proliferation was strongly inhibited by the relationships of extended deterrence established by the United States... and by creation of the nonproliferation regime.*

The second important new challenge is nuclear terrorism. As noted earlier, the concern about nuclear terrorism is as old as the nuclear era. But it has become much more salient over the last decade or so, ever since Osama bin Laden clearly stated that he considered it a "holy duty" to acquire nuclear weapons. Since then, clear evidence has emerged of al Qaeda's intentions and efforts to do so. Moreover, other groups have also shown this interest. This is a very serious threat that is also difficult to calibrate. In the Commission's view, terrorist use of a nuclear weapon against the United States or its friends and allies is more likely than deliberate use by a state. (The term "deliberate" is used to distinguish intentional use by a state from accidental or unauthorized use.) The risks of nuclear terrorism would be magnified by the proliferation of nuclear weapons to states that sponsor terror and the emergence of supplier networks that are outside of the control of responsible nuclear possessors. This is a problem for which deterrence is ill suited, except to the extent that the threat of retaliation imposes restraints on state sponsors. (As argued further below, deterrence by denial of success may have some relevance to this problem.) Nuclear terrorism is also a problem requiring strong international responses, because it requires preventing terrorist access to weapons, materials, and expertise anywhere in the world.

The third important new challenge is the unpredictable nature of the security environment. In the Cold War, that environment seemed highly predictable. The bipolar order, the high stakes, and the enduring ideological confrontation led most observers to conclude that this environment would not change rapidly (an expectation that finally proved unfounded). Today's world is far more complex. It reflects a mix of trends, some positive and others negative. There is profound uncertainty about the future international roles of Russia and China—will they emerge as "responsible stakeholders" or as challengers to order? There is also uncertainty about the future roles of various "rising powers," including some arming themselves with nuclear weapons and missiles. This underscores the need to hedge against the possibility that all of these factors might not turn out for the best and that new challenges for U.S. nuclear strategy might emerge and, indeed, suddenly so.

> *In the Commission's view, terrorist use of a nuclear weapon against the United States or its friends and allies is more likely than deliberate use by a state.... This is a problem for which deterrence is ill suited.*

In sum, during the period since the end of the Cold War, the United States has updated its strategy and policies for reducing nuclear dangers. Indeed, the need for a comprehensive and balanced approach was reflected in both of the Nuclear Posture Reviews (NPR) conducted in this period.

In the NPR of 1994, the Clinton administration embraced the term "lead but hedge" to encompass this agenda. The commitment to "lead" embodied the efforts to reduce nuclear risks through cooperative measures. The commitment to "hedge" embodied the efforts to transform deterrence for different circumstances but also to sustain a force that could quickly be reexpanded if the political transition in Russia took a dramatic and sudden turn for the worse. The Clinton administration also elaborated a Defense Counterproliferation Initiative for the specific purpose of addressing the military planning implications of regional aggressors armed with weapons of mass destruction (WMD).

In the NPR of 2001, the Bush administration also embraced the "lead but hedge" concept, though with language of its own reflecting its own assessment of challenges and opportunities and its own views of the needed balance. It viewed Cold War–era arms control negotiations as inherently adversarial in nature and a potential obstacle to improved relations with Russia. But the administration was highly motivated by the desire to reduce nuclear weapons to the minimum number necessary and to reduce nuclear dangers through innovative approaches to deterrence, assurance, and dissuasion. The Bush administration expanded on the earlier counterproliferation agenda with a strategy for combating WMD through the proactive use of military and diplomatic tools, including, for example, efforts to improve international responses to illicit trade in and transfer of nuclear weapons materials and technologies. It also elaborated a strategy for combating terrorism, including specifically WMD terrorism.

## Current Challenges and Opportunities

In 2009, a new administration has arrived in Washington that has stated a commitment to both elements of policy. In his sole speech as a candidate on nuclear policy issues, candidate Obama made two promises. The first was to recommit the United States to work to create the conditions that might ultimately enable the elimination of nuclear weapons. The second was to recommit to the principle that the United States would not disarm unilaterally and would retain a "strong deterrent" so long as nuclear weapons exist. This is the latest expression of the twin policy imperatives and the question now before the nation, as with each new administration, is how to adapt these policies to new circumstances and to achieve the necessary balance wherever trade-offs are required. What are the specific challenges in the nuclear realm? What opportunities must the nation seize? In the view of this Commission, the following five factors stand out.

*First*, the threat of nuclear terrorism is serious and continues to deserve a high level of sustained U.S. effort. Success in meeting this challenge requires a very comprehensive effort with strong international participation, as argued further in following sections.

*Second*, the challenge posed by nuclear proliferation is also serious. It is important not to overstate this threat because, as argued above, nonproliferation has been successful on many fronts and can continue to be. But it is important also not to understate this threat. If we are unsuccessful in dealing with current challenges, we may find ourselves at a tipping point, where many additional states conclude that they require nuclear deterrents of their own. If this tipping point is itself mishandled, we may well find ourselves faced with a cascade of proliferation.

*Third,* there is a challenge associated with adapting extended U.S. deterrence policies and programs. The requirements of extended deterrence in Europe are evolving, given the changing relationship with Russia, the perception of some allies that they are keenly vulnerable to Russian military coercion, and the perception of others of a rising nuclear threat from the Middle East. The requirements of extended deterrence in Asia are also evolving, as North Korea has crossed the nuclear threshold and China modernizes its strategic forces. In the Middle East, various states depend on the United States as a security guarantor and question whether or how it might stand up to a nuclear-armed regional power. These concerns require a clear and credible response from the United States. Failure to meet their security needs could have significant repercussions. A quick survey of the potential nuclear candidates in Northeast Asia and the Middle East brings home the point that many potential proliferation candidates are friends and even allies of the United States. A decision by those friends and allies to seek nuclear weapons would be a significant blow to U.S. interests.

*Fourth,* China is today of rising importance in the U.S. strategic landscape. The United States has encouraged China's emergence from international isolation and has worked to promote its increasing prosperity and stability for decades. With some success, it has tried to engage China as a "responsible stakeholder" in the international system. But China's increasing wealth has brought with it an increase in its military power, with the expectation of much more to come over the next decade or two. In the Commission's view, the risks of war with China are low, with the primary potential military flashpoint being Taiwan. China and the United States have many differences over Taiwan but Beijing and Washington regularly recommit themselves to the principle of peaceful reunification and, moreover, an improvement in the security situation there is evident. The apparent risks of nuclear war are even lower. But there is also profound uncertainty about China's strategic intentions as its power grows and thus a need to manage these military risks with care.

China does not release information about the numbers of its strategic delivery systems or nuclear warheads. It is reported to have a total stockpile of approximately 400 weapons, of which perhaps fewer than half are operationally deployed. China's defense white papers report that it maintains nuclear warheads for short-, intermediate-, and intercontinental-range ballistic missiles. It currently has approximately 30 Intercontinental Ballistic Missiles (ICBMs) capable of striking the continental United States with nuclear weapons and another 10 or so capable of striking Hawaii and Alaska. It deploys a larger number of medium- and intermediate-range nuclear missiles capable of reaching U.S. allies and friends in Asia (and U.S. bases there)—approximately 100 or more missiles. China says it maintains its strategic posture, including new nuclear weapons, in order to prevent nuclear coercion by others (what it calls "counter deterrence"). It continues to announce a policy of no-first-use of nuclear weapons. But some Chinese officials have made statements indicating that this commitment may be conditional.

China's recent defense white papers have made clear the commitment of its leadership to modernize China's military in order to meet the requirements of "local war under high-technology conditions" and also under conditions of nuclear deterrence. In particular there is a commitment to enhance its nuclear forces in order to ensure the credibility of its "self defensive nuclear strategy." China is diversifying its nuclear missile force by fielding a new set of road-mobile missiles and a small force of strategic missile submarines. Its ICBM force could more than double in the next 15 years. Its lack of transparency about its capabilities and intentions is a source of significant concern, for the United States and for its allies and friends in Asia.

The emerging challenge here is roughly analogous to the challenge with Russia: to achieve political objectives (i.e., engaging China as a responsible stakeholder) while safeguarding U.S. deterrence and also managing the military relationship in a way that promotes stability even as China modernizes, diversifies, and builds up its strategic posture.

This brings us back to Russia as the fifth important challenge—and opportunity.

There are good reasons to be disappointed by the lack of success in fulfilling the aspirations of two decades ago for a fundamental and profoundly positive transformation of Russia's

*In the view of this Commission, the effort to engage Russia remains important … [and] continues to offer some promise.*

relationship with the West. The anti-American sentiments often heard from Russia's leaders in recent years, its use of force against Georgia, and its program of nuclear renewal and reemphasis all raise questions about whether efforts to achieve the desired transformation can succeed. They also underscore the continued uncertainty about the future of Russia's political relationships with the West and thus the security threat it poses.

In the view of this Commission, the effort to engage Russia remains important. Moreover, it continues to offer some promise. President Medvedev appears receptive to the initiative of the Obama administration to "re-set" the overall bilateral relationship. It is important, moreover, to bear in mind that despite our many disappointments, Russia has not returned to the role of the Soviet Union as a global challenger to the United States. It is not amassing military forces along its borders in readiness for an invasion of Europe. Although Russia is strengthening its nuclear forces, it does not appear to be seeking overall nuclear supremacy. Indeed, its focus is largely on its domestic economic transformation and its near-abroad, where there are many challenges but also some opportunities for cooperation with the West. The risk of direct military confrontation between the United States and Russia is much lower than during the Cold War. But the risk of nuclear coercion is another matter. After all, Russia has used nuclear threats to attempt to coerce some of its neighbors, including U.S. allies, and this is a problem for which U.S. nuclear strategy and capabilities remain relevant. It is also conceivable that these assessments might change for the worse at some future time, and the United States needs to hedge against that possibility.

Russia is today engaged in a broad effort to modernize its military forces. This will involve a significant further shrinkage in the overall size and structure of its conventional forces and in manpower levels. It will also involve modernization of strategic forces. It is important to understand the motives driving this effort. One is to replace existing systems becoming obsolete. The other is to try to compensate for structural weaknesses in conventional forces. We note that Russian ambitions to modernize will be inhibited so long as the current collapse of energy prices continues.

The current strategic modernization program includes various elements. Russia is at work on a new intercontinental ballistic missile (initially deployed with a new single warhead but capable of carrying multiple warheads), a new ballistic missile submarine and the associated new missile and warhead, a new short-range ballistic missile, and low-yield tactical nuclear weapons including an earth penetrator. It is also engaged in continued research and development on a hypersonic intercontinental glide missile. If it is successful, this program will result in a more modern version of the existing force with some improved capacity for increasing force deployments if deemed necessary. Whether or when such success might be achieved is a function of resources and political commitment.

As part of its effort to compensate for weaknesses in its conventional forces, Russia's military leaders are putting more emphasis on non-strategic nuclear forces (NSNF, particularly weapons intended for tactical use on the battlefield). Russia no longer sees itself as capable of defending its vast territory and nearby interests with conventional forces. This reflects a complete reversal of the circumstance during the Cold War, when both the United States and Soviet Union deployed many thousands of NSNF. At that time, the United States and its allies were concerned about offsetting the large numerical superiority in conventional forces fielded by the Soviet Union and its allies and built a nuclear deterrent in Europe (and Asia) toward that end. The Soviet Union originally built NSNF for potential use in a large-scale war with NATO and to avoid being seen as inferior in this category of military capabilities.

As the Cold War ended, and as noted above, these NSNF were reduced under the auspices of the PNIs and also the Treaty on Intermediate-range Nuclear Forces of 1987. Nonetheless, Russia reportedly retains a very large number of such weapons. Senior Russian experts have reported that Russia has 3,800 operational tactical nuclear warheads with a large additional number in reserve. Some Russian military experts have written about use of very low yield nuclear "scalpels" to defeat NATO forces. The combination of new warhead designs, the estimated production capability for new nuclear warheads, and precision delivery systems such as the Iskander short-range tactical ballistic missile (known as the SS-26 in the West), open up new possibilities for Russian efforts to threaten to use nuclear weapons to influence regional conflicts.

Like China, Russia has not shown the transparency that its neighbors and the United States desire on such matters. It has repeatedly rebuffed U.S. proposals for NSNF transparency measures and NATO's requests for information. And it is no longer in compliance with its PNI commitments.

Even as it works to engage Russia and assure Russia that it need not fear encirclement and containment, the United States needs to ensure that deterrence will be effective whenever it is needed. It must also continue to concern itself with stability in its strategic military relationship with Russia. It must continue to safeguard the interests of its allies as it does so. Their assurance that extended deterrence remains credible and effective may require that the United States retain numbers or types of nuclear capabilities that it might not deem necessary if it were concerned only with its own defense.

Even as it adapts its nuclear posture to the new relationship with Russia, the United States must recognize also that Russia is a valuable partner in reducing global nuclear dangers in various ways. Russia plays an important role in supporting the NPT and in ensuring an effective export control system in sensitive nuclear technologies and materials. Its decisions on the United Nations Security Council are critical to the effort to deal with compliance issues raised by the IAEA. It may yet prove to be the indispensable actor in the international effort to induce nuclear restraint by Iran.

> *[T]he United States will need to sustain a deterrent for the indefinite future.*

This review of key factors in the current security environment leaves us with two conclusions.

One is that the United States will need to sustain a deterrent for the indefinite future. After all, as this review illustrates, many deterrence challenges remain. Obviously they are not as severe as in the Cold War but there is no reason to think that these challenges will simply disappear in the next few years or that they cannot worsen.

The other conclusion is that Russia, China, Britain, and France have comprehensive plans to ensure that their deterrents are viable for the challenges ahead as they perceive them. To varying degrees, they have put in place programs for new delivery systems and warheads. Some of these programs are intended to replace existing capabilities (as in the case of the U.K.) while others are intended to both replace existing capabilities and create some new ones (as in the case of France, China, and Russia). The United States has maintained confidence in its nuclear weapons primarily through the Stockpile Stewardship Program and Life Extension Program. These programs have been remarkably successful, but many questions are coming due about whether or how to invest to sustain deterrence as U.S. delivery systems and warheads age. The other four nuclear weapon states have faced these circumstances, made difficult decisions, and moved forward.

## An Observation on Nuclear Intelligence

The United States relies on information gathered and analyzed by the U.S. intelligence community to make assessments of foreign nuclear developments. Policymakers should appreciate the strengths and weaknesses of such information. Various commissions have highlighted flaws in WMD intelligence and steps are being taken to implement their recommendations. It is important to bear in mind that intelligence is incomplete on other states with nuclear weapons or fledgling programs—as well as non-state actors seeking nuclear weapons. The United States does not know definitively the numbers of nuclear weapons in the Russian arsenal, especially of non-strategic weapons. Knowledge of possible production rates is also incomplete. There is also less than complete understanding of the activities underway at nuclear test sites in Russia, China, and elsewhere.

*We stand today at a potential turning point.... The world must more aggressively pursue the effort to reduce nuclear dangers if it is going to continue to succeed at preventing nuclear catastrophe.*

## Closing Observations

We stand today at a potential turning point. Further proliferation is possible, which would greatly magnify the risks of nuclear terrorism, nuclear intimidation, and perhaps even nuclear employment. The spread of nuclear materials, technology, and expertise for peaceful purposes—energy production—promises to magnify these risks. A renewal of competition for nuclear advantage among the major powers is not out of the question.

But we can also imagine a far better turn of events. After all, despite many challenges, we have so far been effective in preventing nuclear terrorism, slowing proliferation, and ending the arms race among the major powers. This is cause for cautious optimism. In meeting those challenges, we have learned about the need to be innovative and adaptive, and there is today a rising sense of the urgency of both. The world must more aggressively pursue the effort to reduce nuclear dangers if it is going to continue to succeed at preventing nuclear catastrophe.

Two imperatives follow from this analysis. First, to reduce nuclear dangers, the United States must continue to ensure that its deterrent is strong and effective, including its extended deterrent for allies. Second, the United States must seize the opportunity to lead a broad international effort to reduce nuclear dangers through additional political means.

Toward this end, there is a long list of decisions that need to be taken with regard to the future of the U.S. strategic posture and supporting military and political strategies. We recognize those decisions to be interconnected. They have also proven to be politically divisive.

In broad terms, the United States again faces decisions about how to maintain its deterrent forces. It also faces decisions about how best to prevent proliferation, reduce the number of existing nuclear weapons to the absolute minimum, and provide better protection of weapons and materials so that they are not diverted to proliferators and/or terrorists. Programs to maintain the deterrent force are largely national programs, although their implementation involves a substantial international component with allies. In contrast, arms control and nonproliferation and associated activities are inherently international in character and their success requires the broadest possible international support. This can become important when there are conflicts or trade-offs between the two. For example, a U.S. policy agenda that seems to stress unnecessarily our nuclear weapon posture could erode international cooperation to reduce nuclear dangers. Conversely, a policy agenda that emphasizes unilateral reductions could weaken the deterrence of foes and the assurance of allies. It is necessary to strike a balance in meeting these two imperatives. In following sections, this report will make recommendations for doing so.

In the formulation of U.S. policy, we recognize and indeed wish to underscore the important role of the Congress in the formulation and implementation of policy. Throughout the Cold War, the executive and legislative branches had high-level and sustained interactions on matters of nuclear policy and, although the differences were often intense, the result was a large measure of continuity and indeed bipartisanship in U.S. nuclear strategy. In the period since the end of the Cold War, those interactions have grown less frequent but the differences no less intense. Indeed, the differences have blocked progress in moving to a nuclear posture and infrastructure for the contemporary environment. In order to ensure the continuity of policy that

U.S. interests require in the nuclear realm, serious efforts must be made to renew executive-legislative dialogue and leadership on these issues and to seek a consensus on future steps.

This analysis points to the following findings and recommendations.

## Findings

1. Throughout the nuclear era U.S. policy has been shaped by the imperative to reduce nuclear dangers with a balanced approach involving both deterrence and political measures such as arms control and nonproliferation. Although evolving circumstances over the six decades of the nuclear era have compelled leaders to innovate and adapt, there has been striking continuity in U.S. strategic policy.

2. Since the end of the Cold War, the nuclear security environment of the United States has changed considerably. The threat of a nuclear Armageddon has largely disappeared. But new threats have taken shape and the overall environment has grown more complex and in some ways more precarious.

3. The U.S. strategic posture and doctrine have also changed substantially in the intervening period. The U.S. nuclear force is but a small fraction of what it was at the end of the Cold War and the U.S. reliance on nuclear weapons in national military strategy and national security strategy has been sharply reduced.

4. Nuclear terrorism against the United States and other nations is a very serious threat. This requires a much more concerted international response, one which the United States must lead.

5. Nuclear and missile proliferation could have a profoundly negative impact on the global security environment. The further uncontrolled diffusion of nuclear materials, technology, and expertise would likely accelerate the future rate of proliferation. It would certainly increase the risks of nuclear terrorism.

6. The opportunities to further engage Russia as a partner in reducing nuclear dangers are important and should be seized. The United States must also continue to concern itself with issues of deterrence, assurance, and stability in the nuclear relationship with Russia.

7. The opportunities to engage China are also significant. But here too the United States must balance deterrence and stability concerns with the opportunities for strategic cooperation.

8. These developments in major power nuclear relations and proliferation affect U.S. allies and friends at least as much as they affect the United States. Their particular views of the requirements of ex-

tended deterrence and assurance in an evolving security environment must be understood and addressed by the United States.

9.  The conditions that might make the elimination of nuclear weapons possible are not present today and establishing such conditions would require a fundamental transformation of the world political order. Nonetheless, the Commission recommends a number of steps that can reduce nuclear dangers.

10.  For the indefinite future, the United States must maintain a viable nuclear deterrent. The other NPT-recognized nuclear-weapon states have put in place comprehensive programs to modernize their forces to meet new international circumstances.

11.  The executive and the Congress need to renew dialogue on these issues.

## Recommendations

1.  The United States should continue to pursue an approach to reducing nuclear dangers that balances deterrence, arms control, and nonproliferation. Singular emphasis on one or another element would reduce the nuclear security of the United States and its allies.

2.  The United States must retain nuclear weapons until such time as the international environment may permit their elimination globally.

3.  To address the serious risk of nuclear terrorism, the United States needs strong intelligence and reenergized international cooperation through its deterrence, nonproliferation, and arms control efforts. The best defense against nuclear terrorism is to keep nuclear bombs and fissile material out of the hands of terrorists.

4.  The United States should adapt its strategic posture to the evolving requirements of deterrence, extended deterrence, and assurance. As part of an effort to understand assurance requirements, steps to increase allied consultations should be expanded.

5.  The United States should reverse the decline of focus and resources of the Intelligence Community devoted to foreign nuclear weapons capabilities, programs, and intentions. With some important exceptions, this subject has not attracted high-level attention since the end of the Cold War. As will be discussed later, the weapons laboratories have an important role to play here.

6.  The practice and spirit of executive-legislative dialogue on nuclear strategy that helped pave the way for bipartisanship and continuity in policy should be renewed. The Senate should revive the Arms Control Observer Group.

# 2

# On the Nuclear Posture

The design of the nuclear posture must follow from an understanding of the strategic purposes it is intended to serve. In the prior chapter the Commission argued that the international conditions do not now exist that might permit the United States and the other nuclear-weapon states to relinquish their nuclear arsenals. What purpose then do they serve today? And how should an understanding of purpose guide their design?

It is important to begin here with a definition. The nuclear posture consists of the following elements:

1. The arsenal of operationally deployed strategic nuclear weapons.
2. The arsenal of forward-deployed tactical nuclear weapons.
3. The triad of strategic nuclear delivery systems (land-based missiles, sea-based missiles, and bombers).
4. The delivery systems for forward-deployed systems (including both submarine-launched cruise missiles and aircraft equipped to carry both conventional and nuclear payloads, called dual-capable aircraft).
5. The stockpile of warheads held in operational reserve.
6. A stockpile of fissile material appropriate for use in warheads.
7. The associated command, control, and intelligence systems.
8. The infrastructure associated with the production of all of these capabilities, without which the force will not remain viable, both physical and human.
9. Declaratory policy specifying the role of nuclear forces in U.S. military and national security strategies.

In addition, both the United States and Russia also possess a large number of nuclear weapons awaiting dismantlement.

The nuclear posture is the dominant but not the only element of the U.S. strategic military posture, which also includes protection capabilities, including missile defenses, and non-nuclear means of strategic strike. The focus of this chapter is on items 1-5 in the above list. We note that the United States continues to classify specific numbers associated with items 2 and 5 on this list.

## Defining Criteria

Many of the concepts and criteria guiding the development and operation of the U.S. nuclear force can be traced back through the nuclear era. A short list of these includes the following:

- Nuclear weapons are special weapons and not just more powerful versions of high-explosive munitions.
- Nuclear weapons are for deterrence and would be used only as a last resort.
- U.S. nuclear forces must not be inferior to those of another power.
- Nuclear forces support security commitments to key allies.
- A triad of strategic nuclear forces is valuable for its resilience, survivability, and flexibility.
- The safety, security, and authorized control of nuclear weapons are essential.
- The tradition of non-use serves U.S. interests and should be reinforced by U.S. policy and capabilities.

Updating this approach requires going back to the fundamental question about the purposes for which the United States retains nuclear weapons. In a basic sense, the principal function of nuclear weapons has not changed in decades: deterrence. The United States has these weapons in order to create the conditions in which they are never used. But the Commission takes a very broad view of the concept of deterrence, encompassing many elements.

One crucial element is extended deterrence and the assurance this provides to allies and partners of the United States. As noted in the prior chapter, their assurance remains a top U.S. priority in the current security environment and there are some important new challenges to extended deterrence associated with Russia, China, and proliferation. Some U.S. allies believe that extended deterrence requires little more than stability in the central balances of nuclear power among the major powers. But other allies believe that their needs can only be met with very specific U.S. nuclear capabilities. This point was brought home vividly in our work as a Commission. Some allies located near Russia believe that U.S. non-strategic forces in Europe are essential to prevent nuclear coercion by Moscow and indeed that modernized U.S./NATO forces are essential for restoring a sense of balance in the face of Russia's nuclear renewal. One particularly important ally has argued to the Commission privately that the credibility of the U.S. extended deterrent depends on its specific capabilities to hold a wide variety of targets at risk, and to deploy forces in a way that is either visible or stealthy, as circumstances may demand.

Clearly, the U.S. nuclear force posture should not be re-designed without substantive and high-level consultations with U.S. allies in both Europe and Asia and we cannot prejudge the conclusions of such consultations here. The

*As part of its strategy to assure its allies, the United States should not abandon strategic equivalency with Russia.*

Commission's own consultations on this topic have brought home to us that U.S. allies and friends in Europe and Asia are not all of a single mind concerning the requirements for extended deterrence and assurance. These have also brought home the fact that the requirement to extend assurance and deterrence to others may well impose on the United States an obligation to retain numbers and types of nuclear weapons that it might not otherwise deem essential to its own defense.

As part of its strategy to assure its allies, the United States should not abandon strategic equivalency with Russia. Overall equivalence is important to many U.S. allies in Europe. The United States should not cede to Russia a posture of superiority in the name of deemphasizing nuclear weapons in U.S. military strategy. There seems no near-term prospect of such a result in the balance of operationally deployed strategic nuclear weapons.

But that balance does not exist in non-strategic nuclear forces, where Russia enjoys a sizeable numerical advantage. As noted above, it stores thousands of these weapons in apparent support of possible military operations west of the Urals. The United States deploys a small fraction of that number in support of nuclear sharing agreements in NATO. Precise numbers for the U.S. deployments are classified but their total is only about five percent of the total at the height of the Cold War. Strict U.S.-Russian equivalence in NSNF numbers is unnecessary. But the current imbalance is stark and worrisome to some U.S. allies in Central Europe. If and as reductions continue in the number of operationally deployed strategic nuclear weapons, this imbalance will become more apparent and allies less assured. This points to the urgency of an arms control approach, as discussed further in a following section.

Another element of deterrence, in our broad concept, is dissuasion. In this period of uncertainty about Russia and China and their future international roles, the United States should be seeking to discourage unwelcome competition while encouraging strategic cooperation. Toward that end, the United States should so compose its nuclear force as to discourage Russia and China from trying to compete with the United States for some new advantage in the nuclear realm. The United States should retain enough capacity, whether in its existing delivery systems and supply of reserve warheads or in its infrastructure, to impress upon Russian leaders the impossibility of gaining a position of nuclear supremacy over the United States by breaking out of an arms control agreement. The United States (and Russia) should also retain a large enough force of nuclear weapons that China is not tempted to try to reach a posture of strategic equivalency with the United States or of strategic supremacy in the Asian theater.

This discussion of dissuasion brings us to the related need to hedge. Decisions about how to posture forces for the multiple decades in which they might be deployed involve judgments about the nature of the security environment—judgments that may change over time. The security environment may change for the better, but it may also change for the worse. This is a challenge that some characterize as managing geopolitical surprise. Hedges are essentially insurance against the possibility that such a surprise, if it occurs, will not fundamentally alter U.S. or allied security for the worse.

*It is important to underscore that deterrence is in the eye of the beholder (as is assurance). Whether potential adversaries are deterred (and U.S. allies are assured) is a function of their understanding of U.S. capabilities and intentions.*

Hedging involves creating resilience in the strategic posture. Hedging in the nuclear force structure can be done in a variety of ways. In recent years, the United States has hedged against a possible renewal of competition for nuclear advantage by Russia by retaining a large number of nuclear weapons in the reserve force and a diverse set of options for uploading those onto the existing delivery systems. But hedging is not without its strategic costs, among them the inherent danger of stimulating an unwanted arms race as a result of inadequate transparency.

With those broader aspects of deterrence in mind, we can return now to the narrower question of how to design a nuclear force that can be effective in influencing the cost-benefit calculus of the leaders(s) of a state contemplating possible challenges to and attacks on U.S. vital interests.

It is important to underscore that deterrence is in the eye of the beholder (as is assurance). Whether potential adversaries are deterred (and U.S. allies are assured) is a function of their understanding of U.S. capabilities and intentions. Those capabilities must be sufficiently visible and sufficiently impressive. But deterrence is more than a summary calculation of cumulative target kill probabilities. And it is not simply a function of technical characteristics of the nuclear force. It derives also from perceptions of U.S. intent and credibility, and the declaratory policy that embodies these factors.

In the Cold War, the deterrence calculus was relatively simple. The president authorized guidance to hold a broad array of targets at risk and the military designed systems and operational plans for doing so. The deterrent effect was understood to derive from the expected damage that an adversary might calculate and his uncertainty that he could bear the cost—or even predict it reliably. The United States went to great lengths to ensure that its deterrent was perceived as credible and effective, including through strong declaratory and other policies that in the event would have made it very difficult for the United States to back away from its deterrent commitments.

*As the security environment has grown more complex and fluid, the United States faces a diverse set of potential opponents, circumstances, and threats for which nuclear deterrence might be relevant.*

In today's world, this simple approach is difficult to replicate. As the security environment has grown more complex and fluid, the United States faces a diverse set of potential opponents, circumstances, and threats for which nuclear deterrence might be relevant. This implies that the United States needs a spectrum of nuclear and non-nuclear force employment options and flexibility in planning along with the traditional requirements for forces that are sufficiently lethal and certain of their result to threaten an appropriate array of targets credibly. It also underscores the potential challenges of effective deterrence, as it brings with it more openings for ignorance, extreme motivations, distorted communications, and a lack of mutual understanding. Essential to the future effective functioning of deterrence is that we gain insights into the strategic thinking of the nations being deterred, so that we can understand their motivations and how to communicate effectively with them in crisis. But even with a careful assessment of the pertinent details and context, deterrence is uncertain. All nations, unsurprisingly, seek to protect what they value. And some have expended considerable effort to protect assets they highly value, rendering them vulnerable only to nuclear threats, if that.

One additional design factor requires discussion here: given that deterrence is uncertain and may prove unreliable, the United States must also design its strategic forces with the objective of being able to limit damage from an attacker if a war begins. Such damage-limitation capabilities are important because of the possibility of accidental or unauthorized launches by a state or attacks by terrorists. Damage limitation is achieved not only by active defenses, including missile defense, but also by the ability to attack forces that might yet be launched against the United States or its allies.

## Determining the Size of the Nuclear Force

The Commission was asked to provide a specific number for the correct size of the U.S. nuclear force. It cannot do so. The number is a function of many variables, including the ones elaborated above as well as those elaborated in the discussion of arms control below. The number is also a function of presidential choice.

The size and attributes of the nuclear arsenal are matters to be determined by the President in close consultation with his political and military advisers. He provides overall guidance with respect to deterrence but the specific selection of types of targets to hold at risk and at what level of confidence is a technical decision that would benefit from extensive interaction between the President and the Department of Defense. These decisions must reflect high-level political assessments of deterrence goals and requirements, the circumstances that might lead a U.S. president to threaten to use nuclear weapons, and the outcomes that such threatened use might be intended to create. They must also reflect choices about the objectives of national security strategy and the types of strategic relationships the United States wishes to have with other states, whether allies or others.

Based on the advice of the Department of Defense with regard to necessary targets, the President provides guidance on what principles should guide targeting strategy and the sizing of the stockpile. Such decisions should also be informed by assessments of what is needed for extended deterrence, assurance, and dissuasion. Over the years, presidents have periodically adjusted this guidance to account for changing political and military circumstances. While assurance and dissuasion have been important factors, there does not appear to be any widely accepted methodology for reaching a decision on how many weapons are needed for these purposes. Consulting more closely with allies regarding their views on what is required for their assurance is an important first step.

The required size of the overall stockpile depends on the number of deployed weapons as well as a determination of the necessary ratio of deployed to non-deployed weapons, and the responsiveness of the infrastructure. Once the President determines the size of the deployed stockpile, he will need to decide if he wants to maintain a hedge in the form of a triad and a stockpile of non-deployed weapons that can quickly be uploaded in the event of a rapid deterioration of the international situation. His decision on that issue will determine in significant part how large the total stockpile needs to be.

The Commission's basic assessment is that the sizing of U.S. forces remains overwhelmingly driven by Russia. This is not because we see it as an enemy; it is because some of our allies see Russia as a potential threat and also because it retains the ability to destroy the United States. For the deterrence of attacks by regional nuclear powers or terrorists, the weapons requirements are relatively modest. Even for deterrence of China, the requirements are not large. Currently, no one seriously contemplates a direct Russian attack on the United States. Some U.S. allies are fearful of Russia, and look to the United States for reassurance. With an eye on balance and equity in the U.S.-Russian strategic relationship, it is important to look beyond the balance of operationally deployed strategic nuclear weapons. Russian non-strategic nuclear forces must be accounted for in the overall calculus, not least because of their evidently rising value in Russian military doctrine and national security strategy and because of clear allied concern about this development. We need not, however, seek numerical equality to Russia in non-strategic nuclear forces, as Russia is attempting to offset their perceived conventional disadvantages. We must bear in mind that the ultimate goal for the strategic posture on both sides is to maintain a strategic balance—as Russians regularly and insistently remind us.

What does this imply for additional reductions? Substantial stockpile reductions need to be done bilaterally with the Russians, and at some level of reductions, with other nuclear powers. But some potential reductions in non-deployed weapons need not await Russia. The United States could reduce its reliance on, and thus supply of, reserve warheads if it were to refurbish the nuclear infrastructure.

## On Delivery Systems

In the years ahead, U.S. policymakers will face difficult and expensive decisions about how to maintain the delivery systems for nuclear weapons.

Should the triad of strategic delivery systems be maintained? This triad came together at significant expense through the Cold War and over the next several decades all of it will come due for recapitalization and replacement. Limited life extension programs have already begun. Long lead times dictate that replacement programs start a decade or more before the first replacement systems come on line.

> *In the years ahead, U.S. policymakers will face difficult and expensive decisions about how to maintain the delivery systems for nuclear weapons.*

Given that the triad was designed for a Cold War that has now well receded into history, does the United States need to maintain it? Might a dyad be preferable? The Commission has reviewed arguments in favor of a dyad but recommends retention of the current triad. Each leg of the triad has its own value:

- The bomber force is valuable particularly for extending deterrence in time of crisis, as their deployment is visible and signals U.S. commitment. Bombers also impose a significant cost burden on potential adversaries in terms of the need to invest in advanced air defenses.
- The Intercontinental Ballistic Missile (ICBM) force imposes on a prospective aggressor the need to contemplate attacking only with very large number of nuclear weapons, substantially depleting its forces

while ensuring a devastating response by the United States. The force is also immediately responsive in a highly controlled manner. And for the foreseeable future, there is no prospect that a significant portion of the ICBM force can be destroyed by a preemptive strike on the United States by small nuclear powers, including China.

- The Submarine Launched Ballistic Missile (SLBM) force is currently the most survivable, meaning that no attacker could contemplate a nuclear attack on the United States without expecting U.S. retaliation.

Resilience and flexibility of the triad have proven valuable as the number of operationally deployed strategic nuclear weapons has declined. They promise to become even more important as systems age and if back-up systems within each leg of the triad are reduced. If one leg of the triad were to go out of service as a result of a technical problem in the delivery system or warhead, the other two legs could still provide credible deterrence.

Should delivery systems for non-strategic nuclear weapons be maintained? These are of two types: dual-capable aircraft and cruise missiles. The former are primarily relevant to extended deterrence to allies in Europe whereas the latter are primarily relevant to extended deterrence to allies in Asia.

In Europe, the current fleet of dual-capable aircraft is slated for retirement within the next decade. A future variant of the advanced fighter, the F-35 or Joint Strike Fighter, is intended to be a replacement for the current dual-capable aircraft beginning in 2016. NATO allies are committed to the modernization of dual-capable aircraft and the United States should proceed in partnership with them. The current defense budget includes no funding for commencing the promised production.

In Asia, extended deterrence relies heavily on the deployment of nuclear cruise missiles on some Los Angeles class attack submarines—the Tomahawk Land Attack Missile/Nuclear (TLAM/N). This capability will be retired in 2013 unless steps are taken to maintain it. U.S. allies in Asia are not integrated in the same way into nuclear planning and have not been asked to make commitments to delivery systems. In our work as a Commission it has become clear to us that some U.S. allies in Asia would be very concerned by TLAM/N retirement.

In this review of the future of the U.S. nuclear deterrent, it is important to recall also the serious concerns raised in previous reports about the ability of the Department of Defense to perform its nuclear deterrence responsibilities and the commitment of its leadership to do so. Significant problems with the overall management of the Department's nuclear responsibilities were revealed and discussed in the 2008 Report of the Secretary of Defense Task Force on DoD Nuclear Weapons Management. The September 2008 Defense Science Board Task Force on Nuclear Deterrence Skills was similarly critical.

The Commission endorses the thrust of both reports, commends them to the Congress, and urges the Secretary of Defense to act promptly on their recommendations.

As the United States considers the long-term future of its nuclear triad, it must also address a set of problems associated with industrial infrastructure.

The infrastructure that supports two thirds of the strategic deterrent triad—the SLBMs and ICBMs—is not being sustained. There are no new missile production programs planned for more than a decade and decisions on follow-on ICBMs and SLBMs have not been made. In the interim, the United States has no other missile development programs utilizing solid fuels (currently, its space launch capabilities utilize liquid fuels, with the exception of the soon-to-be retired space shuttle). Assuming the United States is not ready to abandon these kinds of missile systems, it needs to preserve the option to replace them when required. While both Navy and Air Force missile delivery systems are now undergoing life extension programs, these efforts do not significantly exercise design and system engineering. Further, with the possible exception of missile motors, production will soon come to a close. Industry uniformly and understandably emphasizes that expertise can only be maintained with active programs. The skills being exercised today for nuclear deterrent forces are almost exclusively related to the less demanding sustainment of systems first deployed many years ago.

The need for special efforts to sustain key components of the large diameter ballistic missile infrastructure has been repeatedly recognized since 1990. On the present path, in the not too distant future, the infrastructure unique to strategic missiles will not be available for any new programs or to respond to major problems, should they develop, in deployed systems. Any reconstitution of capability (both facilities and people) will take many years.

The solution to this problem will involve programs to transfer critical skills to early career personnel in industry, funding of advanced development to support next-generation system development, and programs to support critical areas not fully supportable by advanced development. The Commission stresses the need for sustaining this capability. A decision to preserve the unique technologies critical to infrastructure sustainment will require the funding of development programs, but not a commitment to full-scale production.

There is an infrastructure issue with the dual-capable aircraft as well. F-35 contractors are not now funded to engage in technical discussions with NNSA's laboratories to evaluate the impact of adding nuclear capability to the F-35. As a result, the current B61 nuclear bomb Life Extension Program study will go forward with limited communications with the designers of the only non-strategic aircraft that would remain to carry it. In addition, consideration of new approaches for incorporating nuclear surety (ensuring that aircraft carrying nuclear weapons meet the necessary safety, security, and control requirements) will be delayed. Historically, adding nuclear surety after basic design of a delivery system has incurred large, often prohibitive costs. Today, modern digital technology may allow nuclear surety to be "added" to an otherwise non-nuclear capable aircraft platform at reasonable cost. The concepts behind this vision cannot be developed without exploring implementation on a real system. Such a prospect was in the offing with the simultaneous undertaking of engineering nuclear capability for the F-35 and the B61 nuclear bomb Life Extension Program study. Delaying nuclear funding for the F-35 will preclude exploring this new concept and increase costs.

As the United States begins to plan its strategic forces for the future, it should take steps to strengthen the associated planning and design processes with an eye to addressing these concerns about infrastructure and deterrence skills. A competitive assessment process should underpin the planning and design efforts. Each element of the deterrent would benefit from rigorous assessment by competing teams of analysts. The organization of such competitive assessments should be the responsibility of U.S. Strategic Command and the National Nuclear Security Administration (NNSA). But they should involve project offices, major systems contractors, and experts from NNSA and elsewhere. These teams should evaluate design, production, integration, flight tests, and field operations. The ultimate objective should be to perform an integrated competitive review of each component of the U.S. nuclear deterrent.

The Commission has not reviewed command, control, and communications. These are important elements of the U.S. deterrent. But they are also the subject of a separate commission.

## Findings

1. The U.S. nuclear posture consists of many elements, including operationally deployed strategic nuclear weapons; forward-deployed tactical nuclear weapons; the triad of strategic nuclear delivery systems; the delivery systems for forward-deployed weapons; the stockpile of warheads held in operational reserve; a stockpile of fissile material appropriate for use in warheads; the associated command, control, and intelligence systems; and the infrastructure associated with the production of all of these capabilities.

2. There is no right number of weapons needed for the U.S. strategic posture other than one that is derived from a complex decision-making process, originating with the president. To determine that number, the strategic context must be assessed. Political judgment

from the highest level of the government is required. Numbers associated with different force sizes must be set in a strategic context.

3. In formulating an overall posture, the United States should employ a broad concept of deterrence. Extended deterrence and dissuasion and the need to hedge against uncertainty have design implications for the posture.

4. The sizing of U.S. forces remains overwhelmingly driven by Russia. For the deterrence of attacks by regional powers or terrorists, the weapons requirements are relatively modest. Even deterrence of China does not require large numbers. Currently, no one seriously contemplates a direct Russian attack on the United States. Some U.S. allies located closer to Russia are fearful of Russia and look to the United States for reassurance.

5. The United States could maintain its security while reducing its reliance on nuclear weapons and making further reductions in the size of its stockpile, if this were done while also preserving the resilience and survivability of U.S. forces. Substantial stockpile reductions would need to be done bilaterally with the Russians, and at some level of reductions, with other nuclear powers. But some potential reductions in non-deployed weapons need not await Russia. The United States could reduce its reliance on, and thus supply of, reserve warheads if it were to refurbish the nuclear infrastructure.

## Recommendations

1. The force structure should be sized (and shaped) to meet a diverse set of national objectives. This requires a high-level assessment of strategic context. Reductions in deployed forces should be made on the basis of bilateral agreement with Russia.

2. Deterrence considerations, broadly defined, should inform the development of the next U.S. strategic posture.

3. The triad of strategic delivery systems continues to have value. Each leg of the nuclear triad provides unique contributions to stability. As the overall force shrinks, their unique values become more prominent.

4. The United States should also retain capabilities for the delivery of non-strategic nuclear weapons and proceed in close consultation with allies in Europe and Asia in doing so.

5. Force posture design and arms control should keep stability and U.S. credibility as their central objectives.

6. Steps should be taken to ensure the continued viability of the infrastructure supporting delivery systems.

# 3

# On Missile Defense

Missile defenses are an integral part of the strategic posture of the United States after the Cold War. Such defenses were essentially impractical before, given the massive arsenal of multi-range Soviet missiles. In the past, they have also been counterproductive in that they drove the expansion of offensive capabilities. Today, the missile threats of most immediate concern originate from countries such as North Korea and Iran which have deployed short- to medium-range ballistic missiles, and are developing long-range missiles. For example, Iran has several hundred mobile short and medium-range missiles that could threaten U.S. allies and bases, and the recent launch of its Safir-2 Space Launch Vehicle demonstrated some technologies necessary for the development of a crude long-range missile. North Korea has hundreds of mobile short- and medium-range ballistic missiles, and has under development liquid-fueled rockets that could serve as a space launch vehicle for a satellite or as a first-generation long-range missile.

Ballistic missile defense capabilities can play a useful role in support of the basic objectives of deterrence, broadly defined, and damage limitation against limited threats, as set out in the previous chapter. These capabilities may contribute to deterrence by raising doubts in a potential aggressor's mind about the prospects of success in attempts to coerce or attack others. They may contribute to assurance of allies, by increasing their protection and also reducing the risks that the United States would face in protecting them against a regional aggressor. Defenses against short- and medium-range ballistic missiles are seen by some U.S. allies as increasingly important to their security. Israel and Japan have demonstrated the value they ascribe to missile defense by joining in cooperative programs with the United States. The Commission strongly supports continued missile defense cooperation with allies. It lowers costs for all and strengthens the potential for collective defense.

The United States has fielded a ballistic missile defense system capable of defending against these short- to medium-range missiles. U.S. missile defense systems in development and deployment, including the Terminal

High Altitude Area Defense (THAAD) system, Patriot Advanced Capability (PAC) 3, and the Aegis Combat System, have had numerous successful flight tests. The United States currently plans to complete deployment of 96 THAAD and 133 Standard Missile 3 interceptors. These numbers should be reviewed if the threat from North Korean or Iranian missiles increases.

The United States has also fielded a ground-based system intended to defend against small numbers of long-range missiles. This system has demonstrated some capability against unsophisticated threats and should undergo additional system testing to determine its effectiveness against more complex threats that include technologies intended to help in-coming missiles penetrate the defense (so-called penetration aids). Further development and deployment of these long-range defense interceptors should depend on results of these tests and on developments in the ICBM threats facing the United States and its allies. Research and development should continue on responses to counter limited but more complex threats.

For more than a decade the development of U.S. ballistic missile defenses has been guided by the principles of (1) protecting against limited strikes while (2) taking into account the legitimate concerns of Russia and China about strategic stability. These remain sound guiding principles. Defenses sufficient to sow doubts in Moscow or Beijing about the viability of their deterrents could lead them to take actions that increase the threat to the United States and its allies and friends. Both Russia and China have expressed concerns. Current U.S. plans for missile defense should not call into question the viability of Russia's nuclear deterrent. China sees its concerns as more immediate, given the much smaller size of its nuclear force. U.S. assessments indicate that a significant operational impact on the Chinese deterrent would require a larger and more capable defense than the United States has plans to construct, but China may already be increasing the size of its ICBM force in response to its assessment of the U.S. missile defense program.

*For more than a decade the development of U.S. ballistic missile defenses has been guided by the principles of (1) protecting against limited strikes while (2) taking into account the legitimate concerns of Russia and China about strategic stability. These remain sound guiding principles.*

The Commission supports a substantial role for defenses against short- to medium-range missiles. Defenses against longer range missiles should be based on their demonstrated effectiveness and the projected threat from North Korea and Iran. Defenses against these limited threats should be designed to avoid giving Russia or China a reason to increase their strategic threat to the United States or its allies. But these defenses should become capable against more complex limited threats as they mature. As noted above, this long-range missile defense system is now incapable of defending against complex threats.

The Commission recommends that the United States strengthen cooperation with Russia and China to restrict transfers to others of advanced missile technology, including the countermeasures to such defenses. Cooperative missile defense efforts with allies should be strengthened and opportunities for missile defense cooperation with Russia should be further explored.

## Finding

1. Missile defenses effective against regional nuclear aggressors, including against limited long-range threats, are a valuable component of the U.S. strategic posture.

## Recommendations

1. The United States should develop and, where appropriate, deploy missile defenses against regional nuclear aggressors, including against limited long-range threats. It should also develop effective capabilities to defend against increasingly complex missile threats.
2. While the missile threats posed by potential regional aggressors are countered, the United States should ensure that its actions do not lead Russia or China to take actions that increase the threat to the United States and its allies and friends.
3. The United States should strengthen international cooperation for missile defense, including with allies, but also with Russia.
4. The United States should also work with Russia and China to control advanced missile technology transfer.

# 4

# On Declaratory Policy

Declaratory policy is a signal of U.S. intent. As such, it plays an essential role in reinforcing deterrence, as broadly defined to encompass also assurance and dissuasion. U.S. intent can be expressed in a variety of ways. It can be expressed as a matter of standing national policy in documents such as the National Security Strategy or the Nuclear Posture Review. It can be expressed in time of crisis, as for example in the letter provided by Secretary of State James Baker to Iraqi Foreign Minister Tariq Aziz in 1990 clarifying the commitment of the United States to react strongly if Iraq crossed certain red lines. It can also be expressed in formal statements at the United Nations Security Council.

The United States has joined the other P-5 states in issuing politically binding negative security assurances to the non-nuclear weapons states party to the NPT. As formulated in 1995, these assurances state: "The United States reaffirms that it will not use nuclear weapons against non-nuclear weapon States Parties to the Treaty on the Non-Proliferation of Nuclear Weapons except in the case of an invasion or any other attack on the United States, its territories, its armed forces or other troops, its allies, or on a State towards which it has a security commitment, carried out or sustained by such a non-nuclear-weapon State in association or alliance with a nuclear-weapon State."

The P-5 also issued positive security assurances in 1995 prior to the NPT Review Conference. They are contained in UNSCR 984, which states that the UN Security Council "[r]ecognizes the legitimate interest of non-nuclear-weapon State Parties to the Treaty on the Non-Proliferation of Nuclear Weapons to receive assurances that the Security Council, and above all its nuclear-weapon State permanent members, will act immediately in accordance with the relevant provisions of the Charter of the United Nations, in the event that such States are the victim of an act of, or object of a threat of, aggression in which nuclear weapons are used."

Some qualifications have been added to these assurances in order to accommodate the competing demands of discouraging nuclear proliferation and also deterring the use of chemical and biological weapons. For example, the United States added that it "will continue to make clear that it reserves the right to respond with overwhelming force—including through resort to all of our options—to the use of WMD against the United States, our forces abroad, and friends and allies." This was justified in part on the principle of "belligerent reprisal," a rule of international law under which the illegal action of an aggressor (such as violation of its commitments under the Geneva Protocol of 1925 not to use chemical or biological weapons) permits the victim to carry out, within limits, retaliation otherwise contrary to its international obligations. This was echoed in 2002 by a State Department statement as follows: "We will do whatever is necessary to deter the use of weapons of mass destruction against the United States, it allies and its interests. If a weapon of mass destruction is used against the United States or its allies, we will not rule out any specific type of military response."

The Commission wishes to make five main points on declaratory policy.

*First*, to be effective, such policy must be understood to reflect the intentions of national leadership. The president must make clear his intent, and it must echo through the words and deeds of the appropriate cabinet officers.

*Second*, the United States should retain calculated ambiguity as an element of its nuclear declaratory policy. Potential aggressors should have to worry about the possibility that the United States might respond by overwhelming means at a time and in a manner of its choosing. Calculated ambiguity may not be wise in every instance, as deterrence in crisis may be better served by being explicit. But calculated ambiguity creates uncertainty in the mind of a potential aggressor about just how the United States might respond to an act of aggression, and this ought to reinforce restraint and caution on the part of that potential aggressor. The threat to impose unacceptable consequences on an aggressor by any means of U.S. choosing remains credible.

The Commission has considered whether the United States should adopt a policy of no-first-use, whereby the United States would foreswear the use of nuclear weapons for any purpose other than in retaliation for attack by nuclear means on itself or its allies. But such a policy would be unsettling to some U.S. allies. It would also undermine the potential contributions of nuclear weapons to the deterrence of attack by biological weapons. The Commission recognizes that, so long as the United States maintains adequately strong conventional forces, it no longer needs to rely on nuclear weapons to deter the threat of a major conventional attack. But long-term U.S. superiority in the conventional military domain cannot be taken for granted and

*[I]t is important that the United States signal in its declaratory policy the fact that it relies less than ever on nuclear weapons for political and military purposes.*

requires continuing attention and investment. This too argues that calculated ambiguity continue as a key element of U.S. declaratory policy.

*Third*, declaratory policy must reflect the central fact that the United States retains nuclear weapons for the purpose of deterrence—to help to create the conditions in which they are never used or even threatened. As argued in a prior chapter, the Commission conceives of deterrence in very broad terms, to include also assurance and dissuasion. Although the contemporary demands of deterrence are much different from those of the Cold War (and reliance on nuclear weapons has been appropriately reduced), the deterrence role of nuclear weapons remains crucial.

*Fourth*, it is important that the United States signal in its declaratory policy the fact that it relies less than ever on nuclear weapons for political and military purposes. The United States should underscore that it conceives of and prepares for the use of nuclear weapons only for protection of itself and its allies in extreme circumstances. The Commission believes that any president of the United States would avoid pushing a confrontation to the point of nuclear exchange.

*Fifth*, the implicit tension between U.S. declaratory policy and its commitments under the NPT to negative and positive security assurances is long-lived and remains.

## Finding

1. Effective deterrence and assurance requires that U.S. declaratory policy be understood to reflect the intentions of national leadership.

## Recommendations

1. The United States should reaffirm that the purpose of its nuclear force is deterrence, as broadly defined to include also assurance of its allies and dissuasion of potential adversaries.
2. It should not abandon calculated ambiguity by adopting a policy of no-first-use.
3. The United States should make clear that it conceives of and prepares for the employment of nuclear weapons only in extreme circumstances.
4. The United States should reiterate its commitments to NPT parties as stated in the agreed positive and negative security assurances, as they were qualified by both the Clinton and Bush administrations.

# 5

# On the Nuclear Weapons Stockpile

An essential component of the nuclear force is the stockpile of nuclear weapons. So long as the nation continues to require a nuclear deterrent, these weapons should meet the highest standards of safety, security, and reliability. The threat to use these weapons must also be seen as credible, meaning (in part) that they must be operationally effective for the intended military purpose.

The number of nuclear weapons in the deployed and reserve stockpile has come down very substantially over the last two decades (with an associated increase in the number of inactive weapons awaiting dismantlement). Presently, the United States retains a large stockpile of reserve weapons as a hedge against surprise, whether of a geopolitical or a technical kind. A geopolitical surprise, meaning, for example, a sudden change in leadership intent in some major country that could pose a threat to the United States, might drive the United States to reload reserve weapons on available delivery systems. A technical surprise, meaning for example a sudden discovery of a technical problem that results in the decertification of an entire class of warheads, might drive the United States to replace one warhead type with another. To hedge against technical surprise, the United States currently retains two warhead types for each major delivery system. This approach to hedging requires retention of seven different types of warheads and a significant number of non-deployed warheads. As the reductions have proceeded over the period since the end of the Cold War, the potential to deal with technical surprise has been reduced, as the diversity of types of weapons in the stockpile has shrunk. Future decisions about the size of the stockpile of non-deployed weapons and about warhead retention are going to have a direct impact on this approach to hedging and may require new approaches.

> So long as the nation continues to require a nuclear deterrent, these weapons should meet the highest standards of safety, security, and reliability.

The directors of the nuclear weapons laboratories are responsible for making an annual certification with regard to the safety, security, and reliability of these weapons. Maintaining a stockpile of nuclear weapons that are safe, secure, and reliable as they age beyond their intended design life is a significant technical challenge. The challenge is magnified in a policy context that requires no nuclear yield from any weapon test. The path ahead involves a number of critical—and also politically sensitive—questions.

## On Reliability

The technical health of the stockpile is monitored under a continuing program of warhead surveillance. When problems are identified, Significant Finding Investigations (SFI) are initiated. In the absence of nuclear testing, these are among the best indicators of the technical health of the stockpile. Over the past 50 years, there have been 1,000 such findings. Over 400 of these have required significant corrective action. The bulk of these have been in non-nuclear components of nuclear weapons. Many result from design flaws or early production problems, although as the stockpile ages, an increasing fraction is attributable to the aging process. Over time, the number of SFIs related to problems of warhead aging is expected to increase. There is also the possibility of new problems being introduced through the Life Extension Program or other modification processes. Accordingly, the Commission supports implementation of an enhanced surveillance and assessment program focusing on lessons learned to help discover and anticipate future vulnerabilities. As part of this program, the SFI metric should be tracked more effectively.

## Approaches to Refurbishment and Modernization

The United States has not adopted the approach of Russia or China to modernization of its arsenal. It has committed to extend the life of existing weapons by selective parts replacement and recertification. This Life Extension Program involves remanufacturing with rigid adherence to the original design. In the remanufacturing process, the only changes allowed to the warhead are as needed to accommodate the dictates of modern environmental regulation and material availability (some materials used in the original production of these warheads are no longer available). This approach has been used successfully. Currently the W76 warhead for the SLBM is undergoing life extension.

The possibility of using this approach to extend the life of the current arsenal of weapons indefinitely is limited. It might have been possible to do so had the United States designed differently the weapons it produced in the 1960s, 1970s, and 1980s. But it chose to optimize the design of the weapons for various purposes, for example, to maximize the yield of the weapon relative to its size and weight. It did not design them for remanufacture. This approach also requires that the United States utilize or replicate some materials or technologies that are no longer available. Designs constraints also prevent the utilization of advanced safety and security technologies.

The process of remanufacturing now underway introduces some uncertainty about the expected operational reliability of the weapons. So far at least, the directors of the weapons laboratories have been able to certify that they retain confidence in the remanufactured (and other stockpiled) weapons. But there are increasing concerns about how long such confidence will remain as the process of reinspecting and remanufacturing these weapons continues. Indeed, laboratory directors have testified that uncertainties are increasing.

This has led to a search for alternatives. A new, as yet untried approach is to redesign an existing weapon to optimize the design with larger performance margins, high performance predictability, and further improved safety and security features rather than maximum yield-to-weight. Such redesign can be done without introducing new military characteristics while improving safety and security, etc.

There are no examples of actually implementing this approach. The now cancelled Reliable Replacement Warhead (RRW) program was intended to do so. The Congress decided not to support RRW in part because of concerns that an untested design might lead to a future need for nuclear testing and that warhead modernization would undermine U.S. credibility on nonproliferation. Congress denied funding for this effort pending a review of U.S. nuclear policy to be conducted this year. In March 2009, the Obama administration formally terminated the RRW program.

The Commission observes continuing confusion about the now cancelled program—confusion that seems to be a barrier to making the next choices about how to proceed to ensure that the nuclear stockpile is safe, secure, and reliable. The term "RRW" is used in different ways by different people. Some use it to refer to a specific warhead design that would replace a portion of the existing W76 warheads on Trident submarine launched ballistic missiles. Others use it to describe an overall approach to the entire U.S. stockpile, a process that would introduce improved performance margins and enhanced safety and security across the board. Some have conceived of RRW as a means of transforming the nuclear weapons production complex, whereby warhead production would be simplified and the use of hazardous materials curtailed. There is also some confusion about whether the warhead would have been "new." In some senses, it would have been new. It would have incorporated some new design features to enhance safety and security and to increase performance margins. But it would not have been new insofar as it would not have provided any new military capabilities. This short review illustrates that, as the nation moves forward, it must be clear about what is being initiated (and what is not) and what makes a weapon "new" and what not.

The two basic approaches to refurbishment and modernization are, in fact, not stark alternatives. Rather, they are options along a spectrum. That spectrum is defined at its two ends by the pure remanufacturing of existing warheads with existing components at one end and complete redesign and new production of all system components at the other. In between are various options to utilize existing components and design solutions while mixing in new components and solutions as needed. Different warheads may lend themselves to different solutions along this spectrum.

> *The two basic approaches to refurbishment and modernization are, in fact, not stark alternatives. Rather, they are options along a spectrum.... The decision on which approach is best should be made on a case-by-case basis as the existing stockpile of warheads ages.*

The decision on which approach is best should be made on a case-by-case basis as the existing stockpile of warheads ages. The Commission notes that several systems, including the W78 ICBM warhead, the W80 cruise missile warhead, and the B61 bomb, will require refurbishment or life extension in the next decade or so. Whichever approach to warhead refurbishment is adopted, the process is inherently complex and expensive. Orderly planning for refurbishment can help to reduce costs and realize other efficiencies.

The commission recommends that Congress authorize the NNSA to conduct a cost and feasibility study of incorporating enhanced safety, security, and reliability features in the second half of the planned W76 life extension program. This authorization should permit the design of specific components, including both pits and secondaries, as appropriate. The objective would be to make the W76 safer and more secure and to provide more diversity of design and reliability for this leg of the triad. Diversity in the W76 is an important hedge against technical failures in the current design, which constitutes a large majority of the force.

Similar design work in support of the life extension of the B61 could follow. These life extension and modernization programs should be guided by the principle of finding the optimum approach for each weapon, ranging from simple life extension through component redesign and replacement through full redesign. As a general principle for subsequent life extensions, the Commission recommends that the NNSA select the approach that makes the greatest technical and strategic sense. Final implementation of the modernization approach for any particular weapon would be subject to Congressional review through the normal budget process.

As the United States proceeds with stockpile refurbishment and modernization, it must ensure that the design, assessment, and engineering processes remain sufficiently intellectually competitive to result in a stockpile of weapons that meet the highest standards of safety, security, and reliability. Toward this end, it would be useful to make increased use of "red-teaming" approaches. How so?

The Significant Finding Investigations noted above have revealed problems originating in all phases from design to field operations—problems that generally have not been identified until many years after a weapon has been produced. The fact that many findings identify problems originating in the design phase of the weapon indicates that original design processes were not sufficiently robust. This underscores the need to maintain proficiency in physics design, component engineering, production engineering, and test engineering. Toward this end, the best approach may be competitive design. For extensive refurbishments or expanded Life Extension Programs, there should be a formal design competition between two teams, a California team of Lawrence Livermore and Sandia Livermore and a New Mexico team of Los Alamos and Sandia Albuquerque. Once designs have been completed, each team should do a "no holds barred" critique of the other design. Production engineering personnel from the production complex should also be involved. This approach was used in the first phase of the RRW design competition three years ago. It significantly strengthened both competing designs, while also improving the capability and proficiency of both the design and production teams.

The concept of competitive design might be complemented by competitive annual assessments. As noted above, each year every warhead type must be reviewed to determine if it can be certified as safe, secure, and reliable by the director of the laboratory that designed it. While it is important that a single director be accountable for these conclusions, each director should have the benefit of a competitive review by the other laboratory. Similarly, Sandia (which assesses non-nuclear components of all warheads) would benefit from a formal competitive internal assessment procedure.

Before closing this section, the Commission wishes to address three further topics.

The first relates to the Significant Finding Investigations (SFI). The discovery of technical problems needing correction, and the process of making those corrections, are treated as routine within the NNSA. But the SFI process does not receive the funding it needs and, as a result, various forms of surveillance have been reduced, including flight tests and drop tests. This is a mistake. In the absence of nuclear testing, SFIs are one of the best indicators of the technical health of the stockpile, and dealing with SFIs is one of the best ways to maintain technical capabilities. Senior leadership, including in

Congress, should track this metric and should increase the priority, rate, and funding of both warhead surveillance and corrective actions.

The second relates to certification of the stockpile. No responsibility of the directors of the weapons laboratories is as important as the annual certification process. Despite this, the existing laboratory fee and evaluation structure takes no notice of certification or its importance. The NNSA should find an appropriate, formal way to recognize the importance of the process. This should not involve assigning fee to certification, however. Doing so could appear to be a government evaluation of the directors' certification, which would compromise the essential independence of the process.

Let us return to two of the concerns that were cited as reasons for the Congress not to support the RRW: concern that an untested design might lead to a future need for nuclear testing and that any modernization of the U.S. arsenal might undermine U.S. credibility on nonproliferation. The Commission is satisfied that the risks of a return to nuclear testing to support the refurbishment and modernization program could be made minimal. In fact, they probably could be made lower than in a program of refurbishment that permits only life extension. The Commission also recognizes the tension between modernization and nonproliferation. But so long as such modernization proceeds within the framework of existing U.S. policy, it should not raise substantial political difficulty. As a matter of U.S. policy, the United States does not produce fissile materials and does not conduct nuclear explosive tests. Also the United States does not currently seek new weapons with new military characteristics. Within this framework, it should seek all of the possible benefits of improved safety, security, and reliability available to it. Moreover, modernization is essential to the nonproliferation benefits derived from the extended deterrent.

*As a matter of U.S. policy, the United States does not produce fissile materials, does not conduct nuclear explosive tests.... [and] does not currently seek new weapons with new military characteristics. Within this framework, it should seek all of the possible benefits of improved safety, security, and reliability available to it.*

The third concern is about secrecy. The United States maintains an unneeded degree of secrecy with regard to the number of nuclear weapons in its arsenal (including not just deployed weapons but also weapons in the inactive stockpile and those awaiting dismantlement). Secrecy policies should be reviewed with an eye toward providing appropriate public disclosure of stockpile information.

# Findings

1. The United States requires a stockpile of nuclear weapons that is safe, secure, and reliable, and whose threatened use in military conflict would be credible.
2. The reliability of existing warheads is reviewed for certification on an annual basis by the directors of the nuclear weapons laboratories. Maintaining the reliability of the warheads as they age is an increasing challenge.
3. The Life Extension Program has to date been effective in dealing with the problem of modernizing the arsenal. But it is becoming increasingly difficult to continue within the constraints of a rigid adherence to original materials and design as the stockpile continues to age.
4. Alternatives to this approach exist and involve, to varying degrees, the reuse and/or redesign of components and different engineering solutions.
5. The debate over the Reliable Replacement Warhead revealed a lot of confusion about what was intended, what is needed, and what constitutes "new."
6. So long as modernization proceeds within the framework of existing U.S. policy, it should encounter minimum political difficulty. As a matter of U.S. policy, the United States does not produce fissile materials and does not conduct nuclear explosive tests. Also the United States does not currently seek new weapons with new military characteristics. Within this framework, it should seek the possible benefits of improved safety, security, and reliability available to it.

# Recommendations

1. The decision on which approach to refurbishing and modernizing the nuclear stockpile is best should be made on a type-by-type basis as the existing stockpile of warheads ages.
2. The Commission recommends that Congress authorize the NNSA to conduct a cost and feasibility study of incorporating enhanced safety, security, and reliability features in the second half of the planned W76 life extension program. This authorization should permit the design of specific components, including both pits and secondaries, as appropriate.
3. Similar design work in support of the life extension of the B61 should be considered if appropriate, as well as for other warheads as they come due for modernization.

4. Red-teaming should be used to ensure an intellectually competitive process that results in a stockpile of weapons meeting the highest standards of safety, security, and reliability.

5. The Significant Findings Investigations flowing from on-going surveillance of the stockpile should be utilized by leadership, including in the Congress, to monitor the technical health of the stockpile.

6. The United States maintains an unneeded degree of secrecy with regard to the number of nuclear weapons in its arsenal (including not just deployed weapons but also weapons in the inactive stockpile and those awaiting dismantlement). Secrecy policies should be reviewed with an eye toward providing appropriate public disclosure of stockpile information.

# 6

# On The Nuclear Weapons Complex

Per the request of the Congress, the Commission has reviewed carefully the state of the weapons complex that supports the U.S. nuclear deterrent. This review has generated three primary concerns, each addressed in turn below. First, the physical infrastructure is in serious need of transformation and the National Nuclear Security Administration (NNSA) has a reasonable plan to do so but it lacks the needed funding. Second, the intellectual infrastructure is in more serious trouble and significant steps must be taken to remedy the situation. Third, the governance structure of the NNSA is not delivering the needed results and should be changed.

## The Physical Infrastructure

The weapons complex includes the following:

- The three laboratories: Los Alamos, Lawrence Livermore, and Sandia
- Four production plants
- The Nevada test site

All of these facilities are owned by the government and operated by various contractors.

The three laboratories are often called national laboratories or weapons laboratories (in the latter case to distinguish them from other DOE national laboratories). They are each multi-purpose, multi-disciplinary facilities with strong general science and engineering components. Each laboratory houses major supercomputing facilities and has unique, large, and expensive research tools. These capabilities are utilized to support the stockpile efforts described in the previous chapter. They are also utilized by the Department of Defense, Department of Homeland Security, and intelligence agencies in support of various other national priorities. (Note that Sandia operates two facilities, one in New Mexico and one in California.)

Each of the four production plants has a distinct function. Weapons are disassembled and reassembled at the Pantex Plant in Amarillo, Texas. Retired weapons are dismantled and uranium components remanufactured at the Y-12 National Security Complex in Oak Ridge, Tennessee. This facility also stores highly enriched uranium, for both the weapons program and for naval reactors. Non-nuclear weapons components are manufactured at the Kansas City Plant in Kansas City, Missouri. Tritium is produced at the Savannah River Site, in Aiken, South Carolina.

The Nevada test site is maintained in accordance with U.S. policy to have the capacity to resume nuclear testing as a condition of sustaining the nuclear test moratorium and possible entry into force of the CTBT. The policy reflects an assessment that the prohibition of testing carries some risks, however slight. Although it is unlikely that a problem will arise requiring nuclear testing, the emergence of such a problem with the deterrent would be a matter of major significance. The NNSA says it can resume testing in 24 months. But test readiness tends to be a low priority for both NNSA and the laboratories

*[T]he production complex suffered a significant period of neglect in basic maintenance. Most of the sites and many of the facilities date back to the Manhattan Project over sixty years ago [and] ... requires significant modernization and refurbishment.*

The Commission's Interim Report noted that "The Stockpile Stewardship Program has been a remarkable success, much more than originally expected." This is true but incomplete. The program has enabled the weapons laboratories to develop some of the capabilities needed to ensure the long-term technical health of the stockpile, including some important new research tools enabling an understanding of the fundamental physical phenomena involving nuclear weapons. But it has generated no comparable improvements in the production complex. Indeed, the production complex suffered a significant period of neglect in basic maintenance. Most of the sites and many of the facilities date back to the Manhattan Project over sixty years ago. The production complex requires significant modernization and refurbishment.

In considering options for addressing this concern, the Commission believes it is necessary to take a long view. Physical infrastructure is unique in the long time scale involved in making changes to it. Although nuclear policy can be altered overnight and force levels can be decreased or increased (to a limited extent) in months or a few years, decisions on infrastructure can take years if not a decade or more to reach fruition.

The Commission considered arguments about establishing an analogue of the Base Realignment and Closure Commission (BRAC) utilized by the Department of Defense to consolidate the complex of aging military bases. The Commission sees such an approach as unwise. There is a simple reason:

NNSA sites are all one of a kind. Accordingly, any consolidation would require reconstituting existing capability in some new place and this would add cost, not reduce it. The specific recommendation has been made by some to close either Los Alamos or Livermore and fold needed capabilities into the remaining facility. The Commission rejects this suggestion, and not just for the reason that it would be prohibitively expensive. The preservation of two laboratories provides competitive peer review in the one area—the physics package—that cannot be tested as a matter of national policy and where theoretical understanding remains incomplete.

*The preservation of two laboratories provides competitive peer review in the one area— the physics package—that cannot be tested as a matter of national policy and where theoretical understanding remains incomplete.*

The Commission considered a variety of studies from recent years about how to update the complex. It is apparent that, for various reasons, none of these has achieved sustained political support.

In December 2008, the NNSA issued its own plan for complex transformation. More specifically, it issued a formal record of decision adopting plans to modify the weapons complex according to a "preferred alternative" which has been subject to extensive review and public comment. This plan would maintain all of the existing sites but would consolidate certain functions, especially at the weapons laboratories, to avoid duplication. Both Los Alamos and Livermore would retain nuclear design and engineering responsibilities in order to provide for competitive peer review. The production complex would be modernized in place, with significant consolidation within sites, especially at the Y-12 facility in Tennessee. Two major replacement facilities would be built. One at Los Alamos would replace a plutonium research and diagnostics facility that is already well past the end of its planned life; this new facility would be called the Chemistry and Metallurgy Research Replacement (CMRR). The other would replace the Uranium Processing Facility (UPF) at Y-12. The current facility was constructed as part of the Manhattan Project in World War II and the many problems and high cost of keeping it running are a testimonial to the failure over the years to make needed investments in the production complex.

The NNSA's plan has merit and should be seriously considered by the Congress. The Congress should not, however, expect that implementation of the complex transformation plan will result in major cost savings. This is unrealistic. Indeed, there may be no significant costs savings. The NNSA proposes to pay for modernization in part with management improvements. But efficiencies may not materialize. Indeed, most projected savings are relatively small in dollar terms. It hopes also to generate increasing income from external customers. But this too will not solve the problem. Moreover, the

costs of transformation will almost certainly rise. The history of nuclear facility construction shows major cost growth. These are sometimes aggravated
by Congressional funding decisions that create unpredictability.

In the past, rising facility costs have been borne by taking funds from
other activities of the laboratories, usually from the scientific base. As argued
further below, this has had a very deleterious impact on the labs and the
practice should cease.

The two planned replacement facilities will be very expensive at well
over $1 billion each. Given the NNSA's historical problems in cost and sched-
ule management of nuclear facility construction, any current cost estimates
should be considered extremely uncertain. Even at currently estimated costs,
these two projects would be among the largest construction projects attempted by the nuclear weapons program in the past 25 years.

This raises an obvious question about whether these two replacement
programs might proceed in sequence rather than concurrently. There are
strong arguments for moving forward concurrently. Existing facilities are
genuinely decrepit and are maintained in a safe and secure manner only at
high cost. Moreover, the improved production capabilities they promise are
integral to the program of refurbishment and modernization described in the
preceding chapter. If funding can be found for both, this would best serve
the national interest in maintaining a safe, secure, and reliable stockpile of
weapons in the most effective and efficient manner.

But if funding cannot be found, what choice should be made? Four factors
should be considered:

- There are safety issues with both existing facilities, primarily due to
  their age. The safety concerns at the Los Alamos plutonium facility
  are at least as serious as those at the Y-12 uranium facility. But a short-
  term loss of plutonium capabilities may hurt the weapon program
  more than a short-term loss of enriched uranium capabilities.
- The Los Alamos plutonium facility makes a direct contribution to
  maintaining intellectual infrastructure that is in immediate danger
  of attrition (as argued further below). It assures that there is a complete long-term capability for Los Alamos and Livermore to conduct
  plutonium research.
- Because the future size of the stockpile is uncertain, projects that
  are relatively independent of stockpile size should take priority. The
  uranium production facility's size is influenced by stockpile size (the
  greater the stockpile size, the larger the needed production capacity). The Los Alamos plutonium facility is required independent of
  stockpile size.
- The Los Alamos facility has the more mature design.

These considerations lead the commission to the conclusion that, if priority must be given, the Los Alamos plutonium facility should receive it. A delay in construction of the Y-12 uranium processing facility may also allow some redesign to tailor the plan to new arms control agreements and their implications for long-term stockpile requirements. The time might also be used to find ways to minimize the facility's size and cost, and to learn more about secondary reuse.

A critical question in the overall plan is how much capacity should be in place to produce new weapons pits. The original pit-production facility at Rocky Flats was closed more than a decade ago. A capability to produce pits has been reestablished at Los Alamos in the TA-55/PF-4 facility. The facility has demonstrated that it can produce certifiable pits and the NNSA plans that it will be the permanent pit production facility with production of 20 pits per year and surge capabilities up to 50 and 80 pits per year. Given the new understanding of pit lifetimes, these rates ought to be sufficient to support the present stockpile or a reduced stockpile if arms control produces such a result.

The Commission notes also a chronic unwillingness of the Congress to support the programs needed to maintain test readiness. This is an essential safeguard of the no-test policy and should be supported. The Commission has also received evidence that some allies interpret the apparent lack of test readiness as a symptom of reduced U.S. commitment to extended deterrence. The Commission supports the principle of maintaining readiness to resume underground nuclear testing and recommends that the program be funded to maintain the 24-month timeline.

## The Intellectual Infrastructure

The Commission's second main concern about the nuclear weapons complex is that the intellectual infrastructure there is in serious trouble—perhaps more so than the physical complex itself. It strongly recommends that significant steps be taken to remedy the situation.

*The Commission's second main concern about the nuclear weapons complex is that the intellectual infrastructure there is in serious trouble....*

It is important to understand the weapons laboratories are more than a complex of facilities and instruments. The foundation of their work in support of the national deterrent is a unique scientific and engineering capability. Although nuclear weapons have existed for over sixty years, weapons science was largely an empirical science for much of that period. Nuclear weapons are exceptionally complex, involving temperatures as high as the sun and times measured in nanoseconds. Understanding these weapons from first principles requires a broad, diverse and deep set of scientific skills, along with complex experimental tools and some of the fastest and most powerful computers in the world. The weapons laboratories also play an important role in maintaining U.S. scientific leadership, especially in nuclear and plasma physics and in material sciences, including shock physics. Academic research cannot operate on the scale comparable to the weapons laboratories and industry has largely abandoned basic research in the physical sciences.

It is also important to note that the laboratories make important contributions to national security challenges other than weapons science. Their unique expertise and experimental and computational tools enable work on many other high national priorities, including nonproliferation, nuclear threat reduction, nuclear forensics, countering bioterrorism, ballistic missile defense, countering improvised explosive devices, nuclear energy and alternative energy sources, and assistance to the intelligence community with advanced technology and analysis of foreign programs.

For decades, the laboratories were places that easily attracted the nation's top talent and expertise in these disciplines. But retention and recruitment of such personnel has grown more difficult recently. With growing frequency, the best of the younger staff are seeking employment elsewhere, and some of the best of the older staff are taking early retirement. Morale and, with it, capability have declined and seem likely to drop further unless steps are taken to remedy the situation.

This problem is aggravated by the need to reduce budgets for science and engineering in order to support the physical infrastructure. The NNSA expects to reduce the number of laboratory personnel funded by the weapons program by 20–30 percent. It is doing so without any understanding of what types of expertise to seek to retain or reduce. It does not know whether the results will be a weapons program too large or too small to meet its required purposes. This poses several risks. The United States could inadvertently reduce laboratory capabilities below some tipping point, after which it would be necessary to redevelop the capability to design and produce nuclear weapons if there is a future requirement to do so, or where it would be difficult to continue to maintain an effective stockpile stewardship program. Conversely, in seeking to avoid this outcome, the United States could maintain more capability than needed, thus diverting resources from other areas. Moreover, not having some standard for what is required leaves the NNSA and the laboratories vulnerable to the charge that they simply seek the largest laboratory complex they can get. A (justifiable) reaction to this belief could be for Congress to reduce laboratory funding in an uncoordinated fashion that would have the unintended consequence of endangering the deterrent.

The situation is complicated because it is not simply the number of people associated with the weapons program that matters, but the maintenance of specific critical skills in a variety of disciplines. The Commission believes that it is important to conduct a rigorous assessment of the numbers of scientists and technicians needed by discipline to maintain and support the weapons program. There are several approaches, including one set forth in the September 2008 Defense Science Board Task Force on Nuclear Deterrence Skills. This effort must provide some foundational analysis on which the Congress and the administration can agree.

Once core capabilities are established, the Congress should require that annual NNSA budget submissions include an assessment of whether the budget as proposed will maintain these capabilities. To monitor progress, the NNSA and the White House Office of Management and Budget (OMB) should establish a formal mechanism for tracking funding sources for the weapons laboratories, without additional administrative burden on the laboratories.

The assessment of needed expertise, its recruitment, and its retention are necessary but not sufficient preconditions for maintaining proficiency. Those skills must be exercised. This is true of scientists as well as development and production engineers. This requires that the NNSA maintain a clear and sustained mission of the meaningful work to maintain the stockpile. This must involve the entire nuclear weapons complex, both the laboratories and the production plants. If further production engineering capabilities are lost, years or decades will be required to replace them.

In addition, laboratory scientists and engineers must work with the actual materials to be incorporated into their designs, in particular plutonium and uranium, to maintain proficiency. Capabilities are not maintained with computers and calculations alone. All examinations of the nuclear enterprise have concluded that there is no substitute for work that exercises the capabilities needed to maintain the U.S. deterrent.

In short, the steps needed to renew the intellectual infrastructure are well understood. The laboratories must be able to provide challenging research on important national problems. They must be able to invest in a sustained and predictable way in maintaining laboratory capability. They must be able to conduct a stable program of work that exercises the full range of laboratory skills. In the weapons area, this includes projects that exercise design skills. Above all, laboratory staff must understand that their work is valued as contributing directly to important national interests.

Recalling the point above about the expanding contributions of the laboratories to activities outside of stockpile stewardship, an additional step might be taken to bolster intellectual infrastructure. In defining the future mission of the laboratories, the NNSA rightly argued in a June 2008 press release,

> "[T]heir future mission is not limited solely to the historic nuclear weapons core mission, but rather is one encompassing the full spectrum of national security interests. The broad range of research and development activities at the NNSA laboratories, which include sensor

and detection technology, high-performance computing, microsystems, chemical and biological technology, and explosives science, will continue to ensure that the nation is equipped to deal with technological surprises and anticipate new … threats."

The Commission has considered various recommendations to formally recognize this fact. It recommends designating Los Alamos, Livermore, and Sandia as "national security" rather than "nuclear weapons" laboratories.

To reinforce this designation, the Commission recommends that the President issue an Executive Order formally assigning the Secretaries of Defense, Energy, State, and Homeland Security and the Director of National Intelligence joint responsibility for the health of these laboratories. The White House should establish an interagency process to accomplish this and ensure that work in defense, homeland security, and intelligence is assigned to the national laboratories, building on work already in progress.

Such a step is needed because that work already in progress has brought home an essential lesson: elements of the federal government outside DOE are keen to utilize the capabilities of these laboratories but they are not keen to invest in the underlying science and engineering that generates those capabilities. As one expert has put it, the rest of the government is anxious to buy wine by the glass, but no one wishes to invest in the vineyard (Frances Fragos Townsend in remarks at the Nuclear Deterrence Summit, December 3, 2008). The Commission believes that this diversification of support is the most—and perhaps the only—effective way to maintain the excellence of the laboratories. But much more buy-in is needed from outside DOE. What is required is not a series of small projects but a few, large, sustained efforts that will support capability building. To accomplish this objective would require strong, high level support and, so far, this has been lacking. The directors of the weapons laboratories have established the following criteria for support from a broader range of agencies: projects should be synergistic with the Laboratory mission, of national importance, and done with excellence using unique Laboratory capabilities. The Commission endorses these criteria.

*The relationship between the laboratories and the intelligence community merits particular attention.*

The relationship between the laboratories and the intelligence community merits particular attention here. For decades, the laboratories have provided unique insights into foreign weapons programs because of their ability to bring weapons design expertise to the study of such programs. As concern about nuclear proliferation and terrorism has grown over the last two decades, this expertise has been in rising demand. But in recent years, funding for this work has been significantly reduced. The Commission recommends that it be restored. It also recommends that the Congress express a commitment to sustain that funding for the foreseeable future, as its fluctuating character over recent years has been a significant programmatic problem. The Commission also recommends that the Director of National Intelligence review and assess the potential contributions of the laboratories to the national intelligence mission and advocate for the needed allocation of resources.

A particularly sensitive question is whether the laboratories should be permitted to do weapons design work in support of this intelligence mission. At issue is whether the United States should seek to improve its understanding of the feasibility of the weapons design efforts of others by replicating those designs in U.S. laboratories. In this Commission's view, this is possible and this work should be permitted. At a time of rising concern about efforts by proliferators to develop and improve their nuclear weapons, and of nuclear terrorism, such work is indeed critical. Such work would not involve the design of new weapons with new military characteristics for deployment by the United States. It can and should be done in accordance with U.S. policies not to produce fissile materials and not to conduct nuclear explosive tests. It would be limited to assessing whether adversarial efforts in development of new nuclear weapons will result in operational capabilities, and what technical, military, political, and other consequences might follow from the potential new capabilities. Working with partners in the intelligence community, the laboratories should be in a position to advise national leadership on foreign nuclear weapons activities bearing on the interests of the United States and its allies. In short, the Commission recommends that the laboratories be allowed to design, simulate, and experimentally assess foreign nuclear weapon designs for the purposes of defensive analysis.

## The Future of NNSA

The Commission's third main concern about the weapons complex is that the governance structure of the NNSA is not delivering the needed results. This governance structure should be changed.

The complexity of the weapons infrastructure and the importance of the nuclear mission demand the highest standards of management and oversight from the Federal government. Despite the efforts of thousands of dedicated and competent civil servants, Federal oversight of the weapons enterprise needs significant improvement. Key to that improvement is reconsidering the role and performance of the NNSA.

*Despite some success, NNSA has failed to meet the hopes of its founders. Indeed, it may have become part of the problem.*

The NNSA was formed to improve management of the weapons program and to shelter that program from what was perceived as a welter of confusing and contradictory DOE directives, policies, and procedures. Despite some success, the NNSA has failed to meet the hopes of its founders. Indeed, it may have become part of the problem, adopting the same micromanagement and unnecessary and obtrusive oversight that it was created to eliminate. For example, in 2005, a Defense Science Board Task Force concluded that excessive regulation originating outside the NNSA but within a risk-averse DOE was raising cost and hampering production at Pantex. An internal review by NNSA leadership concluded that some of the problem lay within the NNSA itself. More recently, there are complaints of NNSA micro management of the new contract at Lawrence Livermore National Laboratory. Outside assessments have concluded that the heavily bureaucratic approach of the DOE/NNSA is inconsistent with the effective operation of a research and development organization. See for example a March 2009 report of the Henry L. Stimson Center entitled *Leveraging Science for Security: A Strategy for the Nuclear Weapons Laboratories in the 21st Century.*

The leadership of all three weapons laboratories believes that the regulatory burden is excessive, a view endorsed by the Commission. That burden imposes a significant cost and less heavy-handed oversight would bring real benefits. This conclusion is backed up by some real data. One recent external assessment of NNSA laboratories (performed by the Hackett Group in 2006) found a very high cost of compliance with federal safety and security requirements—approximately 15 times as much as for companies of similar complexity (recognizing also some important differences in some of the functions of those companies). Some other data is available from a pilot program conducted by the NNSA at the Kansas City plant in 2006 and 2007. Under this program, the plant was exempted from essentially all DOE regulations and additional oversight management changes were made. An external audit documented significant cost savings. Extending this approach throughout the complex is feasible.

Two broad attitudes are often cited as contributing to excessive regulation. The first is the failure of the NNSA and DOE to distinguish between what to do (a government function) and how to do it (a contractor responsibility). This attitude leads to overly prescriptive requirements in DOE regulations and plant and laboratory management and in operations contracts. The second unhelpful attitude is the tendency of the government to respond to problems by imposing new rules that will "guarantee" that the problem does not recur. This is particularly noticeable in the area of security.

In principle, as the Kansas City pilot demonstrates, it should be possible to reduce micromanagement within the existing structure. The NNSA Administrator has, in theory, broad authority over all areas of operation, including the power to exempt the NNSA from DOE regulations and to substitute NNSA-specific procedures. In practice, however, using this flexibility has proven difficult. Some illustrations:

- During the first term of the Bush administration, the DOE General Counsel effectively prevented any NNSA actions exempting the NNSA from any DOE regulations, arguing any such action required DOE staff concurrence.
- In 2005, a Defense Science Board Task Force examined production at the Pantex plant and concluded that excessive regulation originating outside the NNSA in a risk-averse DOE was raising costs and hampering production. Although the Task Force specifically attributed the problem to non-NNSA DOE staff, the department limited its response to an intensive review of NNSA procedures.
- The Kansas City pilot described above was delayed because of concerns of non-NNSA offices over exempting the plant from regulations for which they had responsibility. Although the initial intention was to extend the pilot to other NNSA sites if successful, it now appears this will not happen because of objections from non-NNSA offices.

It should also be noted that the regulatory burden on NNSA facilities is increased significantly by the on-going audits and reviews by the DOE Inspector General and the Defense Nuclear Facilities Safety Board—and also the Government Accountability Office. These burdens are not under the control of either the Secretary of Energy or the NNSA Administrator.

Despite excellent working relationships in some areas, efforts to implement the NNSA Act and to maintain even limited NNSA autonomy have resulted in a large and continuing measure of bureaucratic conflict. This has been a major distraction at a time when the NNSA might have been consolidating gains and realizing efficiencies. Some observers have concluded that the NNSA approach has failed and that some entirely new approach must be found. The Commission has come to a different conclusion. In its view, the original intent of the legislation creating the NNSA has not been realized. The desired autonomy has not come into being. It is time to consider fundamental changes. Organizational changes may not be sufficient for reducing the regulatory burden, but they are clearly necessary.

In considering a recommendation for making organizational changes, the Commission considered a broad set of options:

1. Strengthen the NNSA within DOE through legislation
2. Make the NNSA a Defense Agency
3. Transfer the production complex to DoD while retaining the weapons laboratories and the Nevada Test Site within the NNSA
4. Establish the NNSA as an independent agency reporting to the President through the Secretary of Energy
5. Establish the NNSA as an independent agency reporting to the President with a "Board of Directors" composed of the Secretaries

of Energy, Defense, State, and Homeland Security plus Director of National Intelligence

Option 1 cannot be effective in the long term. The record of recent years points to no other conclusion.

Options 2 and 3 also cannot be effective. The interest of DoD leadership in nuclear weapons and in the weapons complex is, at best, episodic. Placing the nuclear weapons enterprise within the DoD budget may make it too easy to slight long term needs and to use the weapons program as a bill payer. In addition, some observers question DoD's ability to properly operate broad multipurpose laboratories such as these weapons laboratories. Finally, this option eliminates the independent voices in the process of annual stockpile certification that come from involving multiple agencies. The Defense Science Board considered and rejected such approaches in its December 2006 report of its task force on nuclear capabilities. The Commission, with some dissent, concurs.

Option 5 is the most appealing as a reflection of the broader national mission of the laboratories. It is also the option that comes closest to the model that worked for decades: the Atomic Energy Commission. From 1946 to 1975, the AEC provided a clear reporting line: the laboratories and plants reported to the Commission and the chairman reported to the President. It was disestablished when priority was given to the energy crisis of the early 1970s. But option 5 does not appear to be politically practical at this time.

Thus, the Commission recommends option 4. Autonomous agencies reporting through a cabinet secretary to the president are not without precedent and successful models have included the Arms Control and Disarmament Agency and the Agency for International Development. Within DOE there is the example of the Federal Energy Regulatory Commission, which is independent from the department; the Secretary of Energy is in a position to comment on but not disprove the FERC budget. To make this approach work, the NNSA, as an independent agency, should have a budget separate from any other entity. The Commission also recommends that this budget be reviewed by the Defense Appropriations Subcommittees of the House and Senate. Taking this step would be important because it would allow proper oversight of the broad national security functions of the weapons complex as described in a previous section.

Consistent with its earlier recommendation that the President issue a directive designating Los Alamos, Livermore, and Sandia as national security laboratories, the Commission recommends that legislation establishing the new independent agency should provide a formal mechanism for the Secretaries of Energy, Defense, State, and Homeland Security and the Director of National Intelligence to approve the NNSA strategic plan and to comment on its budget in broad detail before it is submitted to the Office of Management and Budget. This mechanism could also allow the various members to carry out their joint responsibility for the health of the laboratories, as discussed earlier in this report.

The NNSA's problems will not vanish simply by implementing a new reporting structure. A major driver of micromanagement and excessive regulation is the attitude of the Federal workforce reflected in both unreasonable regulations and excessive oversight in implementing them. Moving NNSA can only be effective if the NNSA leadership and the Administrator are committed to reducing micromanagement. In addition, the NNSA Administrator must have the flexibility to issue regulations. However, the commission recommends that the Administrator should issue no regulations concerning occupational health and safety but should depend on the Occupational Safety and Health Administration (OSHA) for both regulations and oversight. The Kansas City pilot shows this is feasible. Also, the Administrator should manage a transition over a three-year period to full nuclear regulation by the Nuclear Regulatory Commission. Jurisdiction of the Defense Nuclear Facilities Safety Board and NNSA oversight of nuclear safety should cease at that point. Under this approach, the NNSA would retain oversight of security (since there is no logical external body to provide such oversight), contracting, and construction management.

Those NNSA employees who transfer to the revised organization should be selected, in part, based on their understanding and acceptance of the need to reduce Federal micromanagement and on their commitment to the distinction between the government's duty to determine what is to be done and contractor responsibility to decide how to do it. Changing the culture of detailed regulation will require a strong, experienced, and committed NNSA Administrator. Organizational changes can aid and empower leadership but cannot substitute for it. But success could make a major improvement in the effectiveness of the nuclear weapons complex and there is no better time to make these changes than at the start of a new Administration.

In summary, the Commission recommends that the President should designate the nuclear weapons laboratories as national security laboratories. He should assign formal responsibility to the Secretaries of Energy, Defense, and Homeland Security and the Director of National Intelligence for the programmatic and budgetary health of the laboratories. In crafting the needed legislation, the Congress should include the following additional provisions:

- That DOE regulations will not apply to the NNSA and that the Administrator should issue appropriate regulations without external approval.

- That the Administrator should issue no regulations concerning occupational safety and health but should depend on the Occupational Safety and Health Administration (OSHA) for both regulations and oversight.
- That NNSA will be responsible for all environmental management, including legacy remediation, at NNSA sites.
- That the NNSA budget will be administered completely separately from the budget for any other agency. To implement this separation, the NNSA budget should be considered by the defense appropriations subcommittees of the House and Senate Appropriations Committees, thus ensuring both expertise and concern for defense issues.
- That the NNSA Administrator and the Nuclear Regulatory Commission will jointly prepare and implement a plan for a three year transition to NRC regulation throughout the NNSA weapons complex.
- That once the Administrator and the Commission certify to the Congress that this transition is complete, Defense Nuclear Facilities Safety Board jurisdiction over the NNSA will cease.
- That the DOE Inspector General have jurisdiction over the NNSA. Except for this IG support, that the NNSA not depend for services or support on the rest of DOE.
- That the NNSA should have direct access to the Intelligence Community.
- That the Secretary of Energy retain his responsibility in stockpile certification.
- That after three years, GAO evaluate whether the appropriate independence from DOE has been achieved.
- These changes should not apply to Naval Reactors, which should retain the current procedures set forth in the existing NNSA Act.

Whatever its governance structure, the NNSA needs the resources to perform its assigned missions. The Commission has already made various recommendations with regard to the funding of stockpile stewardship, complex transformation, and interagency support. But a higher-level view of the funding situation is needed. The weapons complex faces some difficult budget choices. If its funding does not increase, the NNSA is not going to be able to realize its plan for complex transformation while doing the needed life extension work and sustaining the scientific capacities that are the basis for not just the nuclear weapons enterprise but the other, rising demands from across the U.S. government for laboratory expertise. On the basis of current budgets, the NNSA is (as noted above) already planning to reduce laboratory budgets by 20-30 percent, regardless of the impact on scientific capacities (and, indeed, without having studied that impact).

A significant new cost driver is security. Costs to protect nuclear weapons and material have dramatically increased over the past few years. Today, security costs at NNSA sites consume one out of every five dollars appropriated for the weapons program or approximately $1 billion per year. Some increase was inevitable in the aftermath of the attacks of September 11, 2001. But in the view of the Commission, some of the increase is not warranted. Both the Congress and the Department of Energy have been reluctant to take actions that might be interpreted as a lessening of security. As a result, the security program has become unbalanced, with few incentives for reducing costs and a tendency to apply standard procedures even when illogical. As an example, in planning for security protection, the Nevada Test Site security force is not allowed to take advantage of the fact that it is surrounded by the Nellis Air Force Base bombing and gunnery range, which has a robust security perimeter. The Commission did not investigate the security costs associated with sites now awaiting remediation, such as Hanford, but it understands them to be high. It expresses the hope that the clean-up of these sites can be accelerated in order to relieve their high security costs.

> *Today, security costs at NNSA sites consume one out of every five dollars appropriated for the weapons program....*

The NNSA has recognized this problem and taken a step to remedy it. A new policy for protection of nuclear weapons and materials was issued in August 2008. Officially called the "graded security protection policy," this replaces what was called the "design basis threat" approach. This latter approach was a classified standard threat, which defined an attacker's capabilities in an extremely conservative manner; sites were required to demonstrate their ability meet this threat. The new approach is more in line with the policies for protection of nuclear weapons used by the Department of Defense and also by the United Kingdom. The Commission supports this decision, although it is too early to tell how effective the change will be in addressing the cost issue. Costs for security are inordinately high in part because of the incentive structure. There are no incentives to do more then simply comply with existing standards and, instead, to use good judgment in the service of innovation. Conditional probability metrics are not being used as the basis for defining the necessary security protection at the sites. A more coherent approach to security will require strong and consistent support from both Congress and the Executive branch.

The Commission recommends that the Congress consider increasing weapons program funding to accommodate a faster pace for complex transformation without adversely impacting funding for the science program. It recognizes that the final decision will need to take account of other funding needs within the DOE budget and beyond.

The Commission also recommends the Congress take steps to make future funding as predictable as possible within the system of annual budgets. Historically, much cost growth at NNSA facilities is the result of funding inconsistency.

This analysis leads us to the following findings and recommendations:

## Findings

1. The physical infrastructure is in serious need of transformation. The National Nuclear Security Administration (NNSA) has a reasonable plan for doing so that should be reviewed seriously by the Congress. But it lacks the needed funding.

2. Once the plutonium pit production facility at Los Alamos (TA55/PF-4) is fully operational, it should be sufficient for expected U.S. needs.

3. The intellectual infrastructure is also in serious trouble. A major cause is the recent (and projected) decline in resources. A significant additional factor is the excessively bureaucratic management approach of the NNSA, which is antithetical to effective research and development.

4. Attracting and retaining the top national talent and expertise requires that the laboratories conduct challenging research on important national problems. This program of work must be sustained and predictable and exercise the full range of laboratory skills, including nuclear weapon design skills. Exercising these design skills is necessary to maintain design and production engineering capabilities. Skills that are not exercised will atrophy.

5. Elements of the federal government outside DOE are keen to utilize the capabilities of the weapons laboratories but they are not keen to invest in the underlying science and engineering that generates those capabilities.

6. The relationship between the laboratories and the intelligence community merits particular attention, given its importance and sensitivity. Some recent budgetary decisions have significantly weakened their collaboration.

7. The governance structure of the NNSA is not delivering the needed results. Despite some success, the NNSA has failed to meet the hopes of its founders. It lacks the needed autonomy. This structure should be changed.

8. The NNSA's problems will not vanish simply by implementing a new reporting structure. The regulatory burden on the laboratories is excessive and should be rationalized.

9. The NNSA needs the resources to perform its assigned missions. Although the NNSA decision to modernize in place is the right decision, the budget risk appears extremely high. The hope that consolidation would save money is unwarranted. Other important laboratory activities may pay a significant price. To juggle all of its competing commitments the NNSA would have to reduce its base of scientific activity by 20-30 percent even in a flat budget and this would have a significant impact on the science and engineering base. The NNSA does not know how large the core laboratory weapons programs need to be to maintain the deterrent.

10. Future infrastructure requirements must be assessed in light of the results of arms control negotiations now underway. Depending on progress in U.S.-Russian arms reductions, some downsizing may be possible.

## Recommendations

1. Congress should reject the application of the BRAC concept to the NNSA. There would be no cost savings and no other efficiencies. Congress should fund the NNSA complex transformation plan while also ensuring that the needed scientific and engineering base is maintained. The plan will not be realized without a one-time infusion of funding above current spending levels and this should be done.

2. If complex transformation must proceed without such an infusion, either complex transformation will be significantly delayed or the intellectual infrastructure will be seriously damaged. If the two major proposed construction projects must be prioritized, give priority to the Los Alamos plutonium facility. In a flat or declining budget scenario, strong oversight must ensure that schedule and workforce issues are balanced in a way that does not substantially cripple current enterprise capabilities.

3. As part of the effort to protect the scientific and engineering basis, the NNSA should adopt a management approach consistent with the requirements of the effectiveness of research and development organizations. A less bureaucratic approach is required. Useful reforms include a realignment of DOE, NNSA, NRC, and DNFSB roles and responsibilities as elaborated in the text of the chapter.

4. The Congress should fund the test readiness program in order to maintain the national policy of readiness to test within 24 months.

5. The NNSA should conduct a study of the core competencies needed in the weapons complex, and the Congress and Office of Management and Budget should use these as a tool for determining how to fund the NNSA.

6. The President should designate the nuclear weapons laboratories as National Security Laboratories. This would recognize the fact that they already contribute to the missions of the Departments of Defense and Homeland Security and the intelligence community in addition to those of DOE. The president should assign formal responsibility to the Secretaries of Energy, Defense, State, and Homeland Security and the Director of National Intelligence for the programmatic and budgetary health of the laboratories.

7. Congress should amend the NNSA Act to establish the NNSA as a separate agency reporting to the President though the Secretary of Energy. The legislation should include the additional specific provisions identified in this chapter.

8. The Director of National Intelligence should review and assess the potential contributions of the laboratories to the national intelligence mission and advocate for the needed allocation of resources. Congress should provide sustained support.

9. Congress and the Administration should also create a formal mechanism (not involving awarding fee) to recognize the importance of the involvement of the directors of the weapons laboratories in the annual certification process.

10. The NNSA should adopt a more coherent approach to security that utilizes tools such as conditional probability metrics to set standards and that creates incentives that are as responsive to success as they are to failure.

# 7

# On Arms Control

T his is an appropriate moment to revisit the potential contributions of arms control to U.S. national security and international stability. There is an apparent convergence of thinking among U.S. and Russian leaders about renewing formal arms control processes and working together in pursuit of deeper nuclear reductions and other initiatives to reduce nuclear dangers. It is time to consider how next steps might best be linked in a coherent strategy.

## The Potential Role of Arms Control Today

Following decades of debate about the values of arms control, it is useful to begin here with a clear vision of what arms control can contribute. Two decades after the end of the Cold War, Russia and the United States are certainly not enemies but neither are they allies. The picture is a bit more complex. The two are strategic partners on some important international questions, but strategic competitors on others. Realism requires that we recognize the existence of potential military flashpoints as Russia has become more assertive in its use of military force in what Russia's leaders call the "near abroad". But realism also requires that we recognize that leaders in both countries have expressed an intent to increase cooperation on the basis of mutual interests, shared responsibilities, and mutual respect. In this context, the strategic military relationship can be an irritant, with new forms of competition eroding the will to cooperate politically. At the same time, political differences are a cause of military competition. Successful efforts to manage political and military relations can pay important dividends. In this context, the potential contributions of arms control are relatively straightforward. It may provide assurances to each side about the intentions driving modernization programs. It may lend predictability to the future of the bilateral relationship, a benefit of value to the United States but also its allies and friends. U.S.-Russian arms control can also reinforce the NPT.

Moreover, at a time when the United States is considering how to reduce nuclear dangers globally, it is essential that it pursue cooperative, binding measures with others. In view of the prospective START negotiations and the U.S. role in extending deterrence to others, substantial unilateral reductions in operationally deployed strategic nuclear warheads would not be wise. The Commission does not believe that unilateral nuclear reductions by the United States would have any positive impact on countries like North Korea and Iran. But some other nations may not show the nuclear restraint the United States desires or support nonproliferation efforts if the nuclear weapon states take no further agreed steps to decrease their reliance on nuclear arms.

> *[A]t a time when the United States is considering how to reduce nuclear dangers globally, it is essential that it pursue cooperative, binding measures with others.*

It is essential also to remember that the arms control process is not synonymous with arms reduction. Control occurs at agreed levels, deemed stable by parties to an agreement after careful analytical work. Any reductions require such work and it has preceded every important reduction so far accomplished. Numbers are not the main point—stability, security, verification, and compliance are.

## Possible Measures

In the effort to renew the U.S.-Russian arms control process, the first step should be modest and straightforward. It is more important to reinvigorate the strategic arms control process than to strive for bold new initiatives. Toward this end, Presidents Obama and Medvedev agreed in early April 2009 to negotiate a new arms control treaty before the expiration of START I at the end of 2009. A mutual reduction of operationally deployed strategic nuclear weapons in some increment should be achievable. This first reduction could be a modest one, but the objective should be to do what can be done in the short term to rejuvenate the process and ensure that strategic arms control survives the end of START I at the end of 2009.

Recalling that reductions in nuclear forces should proceed only through bilateral agreements, the United States and Russia should address limits on both launchers and warheads and discuss how to adapt the comprehensive START verification measures to any new commitments. Success in taking this first step would help create the political will to proceed to follow-on steps on the basis of effective verification.

The United States and Russia should also begin at an early stage to explore the challenges of deeper nuclear reductions. They are numerous. As the number of operationally deployed strategic nuclear weapons shrinks in proportion of the rest of the strategic posture, features other than numbers become more important. The challenges of finding stabilizing, balanced postures will become only more pronounced as deeper reductions require the participation of additional states. Among the challenges that must be explored are the following:

- How should non-strategic nuclear weapons be accounted for? The imbalance favoring Russia is worrisome, including for allies, and it will become more worrisome as the number of strategic weapons is decreased. Dealing with this imbalance is urgent and, indeed, some commissioners would give priority to this over taking further steps to reduce the number of operationally deployed strategic nuclear weapons.
- How should the non-nuclear strike capabilities be accounted for? Under START counting rules, strategic systems are counted as nuclear, whether or not they carry nuclear payloads. This approach could become less viable as nuclear numbers decline.
- How will the theater force balances between Russia and China (and others, potentially) be accounted for? Russia is already seeking relief from the constraints of the INF treaty on the argument that it is unilaterally constrained from addressing the imbalance created by the build-ups of medium- and intermediate-range missiles in states around its periphery, but any renewed Russian deployment of such systems would alarm U.S. allies and friends in Europe and Asia.
- How will the different defensive capabilities of the United States, Russia, and China affect strategic balances and stability? The United States is pursuing a limited defense against limited missile attack and Russia retains an area missile defense system with nuclear-armed interceptors ringing Moscow.
- How will it be possible to verify compliance with warhead reductions?
- What types of hedges will different nations consider necessary and how can they be balanced so that no one perceives a potential disadvantage if competition for strategic advantage should be renewed by another actor?

Simple answers to most of these questions do not exist. But answers to at least some of these questions must be found for substantial additional reductions in nuclear weapons to become possible. Simple numerical objectives cannot substitute for the type of rigorous analysis of the requirements of security and stability that should, as we have argued in a previous chapter, guide the design of the strategic force.

## Non-Strategic Nuclear Forces

To address the challenges of bringing non-strategic nuclear forces (NSNF) into the overall balance, the United States must deal with a number of arms control issues. A first priority is to ensure that the INF treaty does not collapse. For many Americans, this treaty is largely an historical footnote. Agreed in 1987, it led to the elimination of all U.S. and Soviet ground-launched cruise and ballistic missiles with ranges between 500 and 5,500 kilometers. The elimination of these weapons was completed years ago. The INF treaty is far more prominent in Russia's arms control debate. Russian concerns about the treaty crested in 2007 with a series of high-level statements threatening to withdraw. The Bush administration was able to persuade Russia to agree to a renewed effort to globalize the treaty. The Obama administration has signaled its commitment to this globalization effort. Diplomatic efforts have been made to expand INF membership to all countries with missiles of the specified ranges. But this seems highly unpromising, as it would require states as varied as Israel, Iran, Pakistan, India, North Korea, and China to relinquish such capabilities. The fate of the treaty is a matter of considerable importance to U.S. allies in both Europe and Asia, among many others.

*A first priority is to ensure that the INF treaty does not collapse.*

The United States will need to consider additional initiatives on those NSNF not constrained by the INF treaty—i.e., tactical nuclear weapons. U.S. policy should be guided by two principles. First, the United States should seek substantial reductions in the large force of Russian NSNF. Second, no changes to the U.S. force posture should be made without comprehensive consultations with all U.S. allies (and within NATO as such). All allies depending on the U.S. nuclear umbrella should be assured that any changes in its forces do not imply a weakening of the U.S. extended nuclear deterrence guarantees. They could perceive a weakening if the United States (and NATO) does not maintain other features of the current extended nuclear deterrence arrangement than the day-to-day presence of U.S. nuclear bombs. Some allies have made it clear to the Commission that such consultations would play a positive role in renewing confidence in U.S. security assurances.

## On Arms Control in Outer Space and for "De-Alerting"

As part of its work, the Commission surveyed other arms control issues. Two further proposed measures require discussion here.

The first is arms control in space. Russia and China are keenly interested in such control, not least because they hope that such measures can be used to limit U.S. missile defenses. The Bush administration took a strong stance against it. This is an issue that will not disappear. The strong dependence of U.S. conventional military forces on space-based communications and sensors makes this an issue of great and continuing importance. There are other serious civilian issues such as space situational awareness, space debris, and space traffic management that could be used to develop international discussion and working relationships. The actual promise of space arms control is unclear. In the Commission's view, the United States should seriously study these issues and prepare to lead an international debate about how to craft a control regime in space that serves its national security interests and the broader interests of the international community.

> *[A]rms control in space ... is an issue that will not disappear. The strong dependence of U.S. conventional military forces on space-based communications and sensors makes this an issue of great and continuing importance.*

The second is de-alerting. Some in the arms control community have pressed enthusiastically for new types of agreements that take U.S. and Russian forces off of so-called "hair trigger" alert. This is simply an erroneous characterization of the issue. The alert postures of both countries are in fact highly stable. They are subject to multiple layers of control, ensuring clear civilian and indeed presidential decision-making. The proper focus really should be on increasing the decision time and information available to the U.S. president—and also to the Russian president—before he might authorize a retaliatory strike. There were a number of incidents during the Cold War when we or the Russians received misleading indications that could have triggered an accidental nuclear war. With the greatly reduced tensions of today, such risks now seem relatively low. The obvious way to further reduce such risks is to increase decision time for the two presidents. The President should ask the Commander of U.S. Strategic Command to give him an analysis of factors affecting the decision time available to him as well as recommendations on how to avoid being put in a position where he has to make hasty decisions. It is important that any changes in the decision process preserve and indeed enhance crisis stability.

While increasing decision time for the U.S. president is desirable, we are even more concerned about the possibility that the president of Russia might authorize a launch as a result of decision made in haste that is deliberate but mistaken. The best approach to this problem has been and remains to improve Russian warning systems; the moribund effort to establish a joint U.S.-Russia warning center attempted to help fill this need and should be revived as part of a broader coordinated missile defense effort with Russia. Toward this end, steps should also be taken to revive the crisis hot line.

## Requirements of the Arms Reduction Process

Successful pursuit of this broad arms control strategy requires the following.

*First*, the process of strategic dialogue must become far more robust. This is most obvious in the U.S.-Russian relationship, where renewed dialogue seems now well launched. But U.S. allies must also be consulted along the way, and not merely provided advance notification of decisions reached privately by Washington and Moscow. In particular, now is the time to establish a much more extensive dialogue with Japan on nuclear issues, limited only by the desires of the Japanese government. Such a dialogue with Japan would also increase the credibility of extended deterrence. There must also be robust dialogues with other parties interested in strategic stability, including especially Beijing and Delhi.

> *[A] renewal of arms control requires a renewal of (U.S.) institutional capacity. Those resources have been substantially reduced and should be expanded.*

*Second*, the United States and Russia need to come to an understanding on missile defense, if possible. The United States should explore more fully Russian concerns. The two should define measures that can help build needed confidence. This might facilitate and include genuine and mutually beneficial technical and operational collaboration in this area.

*Third*, the United States and Russia should increase transparency on NSNF and identify an appropriate framework for discussion. This process should include close consultation with U.S. allies and recognition of their concerns regarding assurance.

*Fourth*, a renewal of arms control requires a renewal of institutional capacity. For decades, the United States pursued arms control with the Soviet Union by drawing on deep institutional resources in the Departments of Defense and State, the Arms Control and Disarmament Agency, and the Intelligence Community. Those resources have been substantially reduced and should be expanded. The Congress too needs a mechanism to support its effective participation in this process, akin to the former Senate Arms Control Observer Group.

## Findings

1. Arms control should and can play an important role in reducing nuclear dangers.
2. In both Washington and Moscow, the moment appears ripe to renew the arms control process.

3. The imbalance of non-strategic nuclear weapons will become more prominent and worrisome as strategic reductions continue and will require new arms control approaches that are also assuring to U.S. allies.
4. For the United States to reduce its deployed nuclear forces, it is essential to move by agreement with Russia.

## Recommendations

1. Pursue a step-by-step approach with Russia on arms control. This is a process that will play out over years and decades.
2. Make the first step on U.S.-Russian arms control modest and straightforward in order to rejuvenate the process and ensure that there is a successor to the START I agreement before it expires at the end of 2009. The United States and Russia should not over-reach for innovative approaches.
3. Begin to characterize and study the numerous challenges that would come with any further reductions in the number of operationally deployed strategic nuclear weapons.
4. Sustain the commitment to the INF treaty and commit to new efforts to work in partnership with Russia and NATO allies to negotiate reductions in non-strategic nuclear forces.
5. Develop and pursue options for advancing U.S. interests in stability in outer space and in increasing warning and decision-time. The options should include the possibility of negotiated measures.
6. Take the lead in renewing strategic dialogue with a broad set of states interested in strategic stability, including not just Russia and China but also U.S. allies in both Europe and Asia.
7. Work to come to an understanding with Moscow on missile defense, if possible. The United States should explore more fully Russian concerns. The two should define measures that can help build needed confidence. Pursue possible technical and operational collaboration in this area where mutually beneficial. Revive the moribund effort to establish a joint warning center.
8. Reinvest in the institutional capacities needed to define and implement effective arms control strategies. The pattern of underinvestment over the last two decades must be reversed.

# 8

# On Nonproliferation

Just as this is an opportune moment to renew U.S.-Russian arms control, this moment is ripe for efforts to reenergize the global nonproliferation effort. Concern about a potential proliferation tipping point has mounted sharply and the 2010 NPT review conference looms as a significant potential turning point. The sense of urgency is only magnified by the clear risk that further proliferation increases the likelihood of nuclear terrorism through theft, diversion, or out-right transfer or even sale of nuclear weapons materials, technologies, or weapons themselves to terrorists. As argued in

> *[T]he Commission sees both U.S. extended deterrence guarantees and the global treaty regime as integral to the achievement of U.S. nonproliferation objectives.*

chapter 1, the Commission sees both U.S. extended deterrence guarantees and the global treaty regime as integral to the achievement of U.S. nonproliferation objectives.

The key message from the Commission on nonproliferation is that U.S. leadership is imperative. Some have characterized the effort to bring order to the global nuclear challenge as "America's special project." The continued American commitment to leadership of the nonproliferation effort has been questioned by some in recent years. There should be no doubt on this point whatsoever. That leadership must come from the top. The President should use his "bully pulpit" to lay out an agenda, just as he should use that "pulpit" to lay out an agenda to support the deterrent. His early conversations with President Medvedev and his speech in Prague, on April 5, 2009, are first steps in this direction. President Obama should continue to invest this agenda with the political capital of his administration and return periodically to the issues to demonstrate continuity of commitment. He should also ensure that his administration pursues a coherent and balanced approach to the entire strategy for nuclear security. Good leadership requires setting the example.

# Defining an Agenda

The opportunities are numerous for seizing leadership and include the following:

- Renew multifaceted diplomatic activity and engagement.
- Strengthen the International Atomic Energy Agency.
- Lead a global initiative on transparency, addressing both warheads and stockpiles, with the United States leading by example.
- Seek a treaty that ends the production of fissile material for weapons purposes.
- Augment funding for threat reduction activities that strengthen controls and eliminates materials at vulnerable nuclear sites.
- Develop international approaches to future nuclear energy production that minimize proliferation risks.
- Prepare to play a leadership role at the 2010 NPT review conference.

## Renew Multifaceted Diplomatic Activity and Engagement

The advent of a new administration in Washington brings with it the opportunity to reprioritize and refocus diplomatic activity. In particular, the Obama administration has arrived with a commitment to engage directly with both North Korea and Iran on the premise that such action may terminate their nuclear weapons activities. If these efforts fail, we might then have reached a point where the nonproliferation regime is substantially if not fatally injured. If they succeed, this would have a very positive impact on global perceptions of the future proliferation dynamic. While engaging with Iran and North Korea, the United States must coordinate with its friends and allies, other governments, and international institutions to craft the proper mix of incentives and disincentives to positively influence Iranian and North Korean decision making.

*[T]he United States should also maintain the goal of the talks on denuclearization of the entire [Korean] peninsula and do nothing that seems to accept North Korea's status as a nuclear power.*

With regard to North Korea, it is urgent to complete the disablement phase of the six-party agreement and then move to the effort to dismantle the existing reactor. But the United States should also maintain the goal of the talks on denuclearization of the entire peninsula and do nothing that seems to accept North Korea's status as a nuclear power.

With regard to Iran, the United States should become fully engaged with international partners in talks seeking a political agreement that is acceptable to all parties. The EU and Russia are essential to this challenge, and China could also play a constructive role. The United States and its partners and allies must also prepare for the possibility that such an agreement will not prove possible.

Diplomatic reengagement should not be limited to North Korea and Iran, however. The nonproliferation regime encompasses a large set of agreements, processes, and institutions, and they all deserve sustained and high-level attention from the United States. We should also recognize the role that U.S. foreign policy more broadly speaking plays in helping to create the conditions that might ultimately enable the global elimination of nuclear weapons. Without a fundamental transformation of international politics there will be no elimination of the conditions that cause some states and terrorists to seek nuclear weapons.

Diplomatic efforts can also help to counter proliferation where efforts to prevent it have proven unsuccessful. Efforts such as the Proliferation Security Initiative and the Global Initiative to Combat Nuclear Terrorism are political activities among states that help to prevent smuggling and increase capacities for other forms of protection. These measures complement the NPT by increasing the risks that would-be proliferators might be exposed and unsuccessful.

## Strengthen the International Atomic Energy Agency

The IAEA is the world's watchdog against the diversion of peaceful nuclear technologies and material for illicit weapons purposes. Yet the agency's safeguards budget is less than that of the police budget of Vienna, Austria, where the IAEA is headquartered. The current disparity between the agency's resources and workload must be remedied. This disparity will only grow if nuclear power usage grows as some predict. One panel of IAEA-commissioned experts last year recommended a one-time injection of approximately $100 million to the agency's Safeguards Analytical Laboratory and Incident and Emergency Response Center. Such funding would help the agency bolster its technical and human capital. That panel also urged annual budget increases equivalent to roughly $60 million, from its current base of approximately $385 million. The United States should lead the effort to make this so. The United States should persuade the IAEA Board of Governors to increase funding for the agency. It should also make adherence to the Additional Protocol (which provides for strengthened safeguards) a condition of nuclear supply to recipients. The IAEA should also be authorized to identify nuclear security weaknesses and illegal weapons activities inside countries and charged with responsibility to create an international nuclear materials database. The United States should encourage proposals by other interested parties to strengthen the IAEA and especially the process by which it coordinates its actions with the United Nations Security Council to deal with concerns about compliance.

## Lead a Global Initiative on Transparency

As the two countries with the vast majority of the world's nuclear weapons, and with large nuclear weapons complexes, the United States and Russia have a shared responsibility to increase nuclear transparency and to set a high standard in their own postures. Transparency will be essential to continued progress in nuclear arms control and nonproliferation, as new forms will be needed to address both delivery systems and warheads. The United States should pursue reciprocal nuclear transparency and accounting mechanisms on nuclear warheads and fissile materials, whatever the verification measures agreed with Russia for a START follow-on treaty. The United States could start by securing an agreement with Russia to report regularly on their nuclear inventories and total annual nuclear weapons spending, and then invite the other nuclear weapon states to do the same. It would be desirable to resume reporting on yearly warhead dismantlements, suspended after 1999, which could aid U.S. diplomacy to validate its NPT Article VI progress.

## Seek a Fissile Material Cutoff Treaty

Negotiation and entry into force of a ban on the production of fissile material for weapons purposes would be a valuable addition to the global nonproliferation regime. The amount of fissile material available globally for weapons is enormous and any further growth is adverse to U.S. security interests. The countries known to be currently producing fissile material for weapons are India and Pakistan; Israel too may be producing such material. France, Russia, the United Kingdom, and the United States have all publicly declared voluntary moratoria, while China has reportedly intimated that it has stopped such production. A well crafted Fissile Material Cut-Off Treaty (FMCT) would impose few burdens on the United States, solidify China's stated moratorium, and rein in worrisome arms production in South Asia. Verification would be difficult. But the United States should explore a treaty with strong verification mechanisms. India and Pakistan, and perhaps also Israel, may be reluctant in the near term to join an FMCT and this could delay its entry into force. The United States should take the lead in codifying the existing voluntary moratoria until a formal treaty can be brought into force.

*Negotiation and entry into force of a ban on the production of fissile material for weapons purposes would be a valuable addition to the global nonproliferation regime.*

## Augment Funding for Threat Reduction Activities

The surest way to prevent nuclear terrorism is to deny terrorist acquisitions of nuclear weapons or fissile materials. In some countries these are stored at sites that are vulnerable to intrusion by terrorists or special operations forces. There may also be vulnerabilities to criminal diversion. An accelerated campaign to close or secure the world's most vulnerable nuclear sites as quickly as possible should be a top national priority. This would build on and expand the important foundation of work begun under the Nunn-Lugar Cooperative Threat Reduction Program. Stopping proliferation at its source promises to be more effective than relying on efforts to interdict it in transit. By one estimate, an investment of $5 billion could remove or secure all fissile material at vulnerable sites worldwide in four years. If this is true, it is a small investment for dramatically decreasing the prospects of terrorist nuclear acquisition. Aside from increased financial assistance and political will, the effort to deny terrorists nuclear weapons or materials would be aided by the international establishment of priorities and physical security standards. UN Security Council Resolution (UNSCR) 1540 obligates all countries to adopt and enforce "appropriate effective" measures to account for and secure fissile materials but no agreement exists on what constitutes "appropriate effective." The United States should take the lead on this issue and redouble efforts to provide support for implementation of UNSCR 1540 around the world.

*The surest way to prevent nuclear terrorism is to deny terrorist acquisitions of nuclear weapons or fissile materials.*

## Develop Approaches to Nuclear Energy that Limit Proliferation Risks

Nuclear power stations are now in construction in a dozen countries and other governments are considering the nuclear energy option. Growing reliance on nuclear energy will bring with it a sharp rise in the number of facilities using and producing fissile materials, a much broader trade in the associated technologies, and a further globalization of nuclear expertise. This will inevitably increase the risks of possible diversion to illicit purposes. Steps are urgently needed to ensure that these new facilities and materials are safely controlled, with the hope that this will minimize risks. Proposals to establish an international fuel bank, provide fuel-supply assurances, and create multinational enrichment and reprocessing facilities attracted strong interest internationally, while also encountering resistance in some quarters. They may need to be reconsidered in the context of an integrated solution to the challenge of reconciling nuclear energy and nonproliferation objectives.

The United States needs to revitalize this effort. This should be guided by the following principles. Governments should agree to limit access to enrichment and reprocessing technologies, and the facilities that employ them, to the maximum extent possible. They should find means to assure a guaranteed supply of cradle-to-grave fuel services to all governments that comply with international nonproliferation norms, so that nations have an incentive to forego enrichment and reprocessing facilities.

## Prepare to Play a Leadership Role at the 2010 NPT Review Conference

This review conference could prove to be a turning point in the global nonproliferation effort. It may be a turning point to renewal. But it may also be a turning point to collapse. Collapse would significantly impair the ability of the United States to pursue the agenda reflected in this report for reducing nuclear dangers and would likely create new nuclear dangers to the United States and its allies and friends. Given the U.S. stake in the outcome, a serious, high-level effort is needed to ensure that the conference becomes a stepping stone to renewal. Toward this end, the United States can take a number of useful steps beyond those already elaborated here.

*The United States should reaffirm its commitment to end the arms race and work to create the conditions that might enable nuclear disarmament.*

*First* and foremost, the United States needs to identify practical means for improving the effectiveness of the treaty and Security Council in dealing with noncompliance by states parties.

*Second*, the United States should reaffirm its Article IV commitment to facilitate material and technical support for the nuclear programs of other countries, while clearly stating that the right to such technology is expressly conditioned to be confined to the peaceful uses of nuclear energy.

*Third*, the United States should address Article VI directly and forcefully. Doing so involves making two basic points. The United States should reaffirm its commitment to end the arms race and work to create the conditions that might enable nuclear disarmament in the context of general and complete disarmament. It should also clearly articulate its progress in implementing this commitment by ending the Cold War arms race, reducing the size of its nuclear forces and also its reliance on them, working to prevent and roll back proliferation, and otherwise to promote the resolution of conflicts. It is also true that the United States and Russia still account for an estimated 95 percent of nuclear weapons worldwide. A way forward on START is needed and would be politically useful prior to expiration of START I and to the NPT review conference, as this would be a signal of a shared commitment by Washington and Moscow to continue the reductions process in a predictable and verifiable way.

*Fourth*, the United States and Russia should lead an effort to increase global nuclear transparency. As argued above, this should begin with a bilateral agreement on increased transparency about their own deployed and reserve warheads.

*Fifth*, the United States should define an agenda of specific actions that can be taken at this time and over the next five years (in anticipation of the 2015 NPT review conference) to strengthen the regime. That agenda should encompass unilateral actions to strengthen nonproliferation, bilateral measures with Russia, multilateral actions that may not be entirely global, and actions by all states parties to the regime. The building blocks of such an agenda are evident throughout this report.

The Commission is divided over the value of reengaging directly on the practical steps toward disarmament agreed at the 2000 NPT review conference. With an eye toward reiterating and updating their Article VI commitments, in May 2000 the nuclear-weapon states agreed to a 13-point program of action. These steps did not gain the political support of the Bush administration on the argument that they were not practical or not desirable from the perspective of U.S. national security. Today, some of the "practical steps" are outdated, such as the commitment to preserve the Anti-Ballistic Missile Treaty or to conclude a FMCT by 2005. Others have been implemented, such as continuation of the moratorium on nuclear weapon test explosions. Still others have proven impossible to achieve, such as the engagement of all nuclear weapon states in the arms control process.

The Commission particularly endorses renewed efforts in support of further development of verification capabilities that will be required to provide assurance of compliance with arms control. It recommends that the United States provide significant new R&D funding of approximately $100 million per year on verification.

The first of the agreed practical steps at the 2000 NPT review conference was ratification and entry into force of the CTBT. This is the focus of the following chapter of this report.

## Findings

1. This is an opportune moment to reenergize nonproliferation. Both domestic and international conditions are favorable.
2. Despite the occasional failure of nonproliferation, the historical track record is good and we hope to find continued success in the years ahead. But the stakes are rising and we may be on the brink of a

new cascade of proliferation. This underscores the urgency of acting now.

3. Success in advancing U.S. nonproliferation interests requires U.S. leadership. Leadership requires leading by example.

4. Growing reliance on nuclear energy will bring with it a sharp rise in the number of facilities using and producing fissile materials, a much broader trade in the associated technologies, and a further globalization of nuclear expertise. This will inevitably increase the risks of possible diversion to illicit purposes.

## Recommendations

1. Renew multifaceted diplomatic activity and engagement.

2. Strengthen the International Atomic Energy Agency. Stronger financial, technical, and political support for the IAEA by the United States and from its Board of Governors could enhance its ability to perform its unique and important mission.

3. Working in partnership with Russia, the United States should lead a global initiative on transparency, addressing both warheads and stockpiles.

4. Seek a treaty that ends the production of fissile material for weapons purposes and pursue verification provisions that enable its effective implementation.

5. Augment funding for threat reduction activities that strengthen controls at vulnerable nuclear sites.

6. Develop international approaches to future nuclear energy production that minimize proliferation risks.

7. Prepare to play a leadership role at the 2010 NPT review conference.

8. Publicize more effectively the steps the United States has already taken to meet its Article VI commitments.

# 9

# On the Comprehensive Test Ban Treaty

The Commission is divided over whether the United States should ratify the Comprehensive Test Ban Treaty. When the U.S. Senate first considered ratification of the treaty a decade ago, individual members of this Commission expressed different views of the treaty, and these remain. Our differences come down to different perspectives on the benefits, costs, and risks of the treaty. The accompanying boxed text lays out the key arguments of supporters and opponents of U.S. ratification of the CTBT.

---

## The Case Made By Supporters of CTBT Ratification

Those on the Commission advocating CTBT ratification believe passage of the treaty will enhance U.S. security and increase the effectiveness of efforts to prevent nuclear weapons proliferation and use. In support of this view, these Commissioners make the following main arguments.

*First,* knowledge gained from past nuclear tests and the Stockpile Stewardship Program ensure that the United States can maintain a safe, secure, and reliable nuclear weapons stockpile without additional testing. Indeed, U.S. policy is not to test, so CTBT ratification would not affect current or planned stockpile work. The Stockpile Stewardship Program's extensive computational, experimental, and diagnostic tools will ensure the stockpile under the CTBT, just as we are now confident that it can support modifications of existing weapons to increase their safety, security, and reliability without resuming testing. The role of nuclear weapons in U.S. policy, as described in this report, does not require developing new types of weapons that might require testing.

*Continued >*

---

*Second*, strong support of the Stockpile Stewardship Program and the nuclear complex as a whole is necessary and sufficient to ensure that warhead safety and reliability can be maintained under the CTBT. A key component of that assurance is constant, vigilant assessment of the stockpile's health through the stewardship measures endorsed by the Commission to ensure timely detection and resolution of any potential problems.

The CTBT has a withdrawal option. The United States would leave the treaty if testing were required to maintain U.S. warhead safety and reliability.

*Third*, foreign nuclear programs would pose far greater threats to U.S. security without a CTBT than with a CTBT. Absent the treaty, other states could develop and test new or improved weapons without constraints. A National Academy of Sciences panel in 2002 concluded as follows:

> "The worst-case scenario under a no-CTBT regime poses far bigger threats to U.S. security—sophisticated nuclear weapons in the hands of many more adversaries—than the worst-case scenario of clandestine testing in a CTBT regime, within the constraints posed by the monitoring system."

*Fourth*, the CTBT is effectively verifiable. Concerns about militarily significant tests that might elude detection are overstated. Verification capabilities, including those of the International Monitoring System, are improving and superior to when the Senate in October 1999 previously considered ratification. Potential violators could extract only limited, if any, military value from clandestine testing at undetectable levels. While obtaining P-5 agreement on prohibited activities is important, CTBT entry into force would provide additional authority and measures, such as possible on-site inspections, to clarify and investigate suspicious events.

*Fifth*, CTBT ratification would greatly enhance essential U.S. leadership in preserving and strengthening the NPT by demonstrating our commitment to the NPT Article VI obligation to end the nuclear arms race.

*Sixth*, other CTBT holdouts likely would be influenced by U.S. ratification, especially if there was a major diplomatic effort to secure additional ratifications. China maintains it supports the treaty and, as a result, we believe China is likely to follow the U.S. lead and ratify. Pressure would increase on India and Pakistan to not test and to join the treaty. Such developments would contribute to global nonproliferation efforts even if the CTBT did not come into force quickly

# The Case Made by Opponents of CTBT Ratification

Those on the Commission opposing CTBT ratification believe passage of the treaty would confer no substantive benefits for the country's nuclear posture and would pose security risks. In support of this view, these Commissioners make the following main arguments.

*First*, there is no demonstrated linkage between the absence of U.S. testing and non-proliferation. Indeed, South Africa and several other countries gave up nuclear weapons when the United States was testing, while India, Pakistan and North Korea proceeded with nuclear weapons programs after we ceased. Ratification would not dampen North Korea's or Iran's nuclear programs, and the CTBT would not prevent other countries from developing basic nuclear weapons because testing is unnecessary.

*Second*, the United States would follow the letter of CTBT restrictions, although the treaty is unlikely ever to take effect. Entry into force would require many other countries to sign and ratify, including North Korea, Iran, Pakistan, India, China, Israel, and Egypt—the probability of which is near zero. Consequently, the U.S. would be bound by restrictions that other key countries could ignore.

*Third*, the treaty remarkably does not define a nuclear test. In practice this allows different interpretations of its prohibitions and asymmetrical restrictions. The strict U.S. interpretation precludes tests that produce nuclear yield. However, other countries with different interpretations could conduct tests with hundreds of tons of nuclear yield—allowing them to develop or advance nuclear capabilities with low-yield, enhanced radiation, and electro-magnetic-pulse. Apparently Russia and possibly China are conducting low yield tests. This is quite serious because Russian and Chinese doctrine highlights tactical nuclear warfighting. With no agreed definition, U.S. relative understanding of these capabilities would fall further behind over time and undermine our capability to deter tactical threats against allies.

*Fourth*, the CTBT's problems cannot be fixed by an agreement that all parties follow a zero-yield prohibition because it would be wholly unverifiable. Countries could still undertake significant undetected testing. The National Academy of Sciences concluded that underground nuclear explosions with yields up to 1 or 2 kilotons may be hidden. Consequently, even a "zero-yield" CTBT could not prevent countries from testing to develop new nuclear warfighting capabilities or improve existing capabilities.

*Continued >*

*Fifth*, the CTBT's on-site verification provisions cannot fix these problems. Instead, they seem designed to preclude the possibility of inspections by requiring the approval of 30 members of the Executive Council when only 10 of its 51 members would be from North America and Western Europe. Worse yet, the CTBT allows each country to declare numerous sites with a total of 50 square kilometers out of bounds to on-site inspection.

*Sixth*, maintaining a safe, reliable nuclear stockpile in the absence of testing entails real technical risks that cannot be eliminated by even the most sophisticated science-based program because full validation of these programs is likely to require testing over time. With nuclear arms reductions our confidence in each weapon becomes paramount, but CTBT ratification would foreclose means to that confidence.

In short, under the CTBT, opponents could make improvements in their nuclear capabilities while U.S. ratification would preclude the testing that could help preserve the U.S. capability to deter them. Given these serious problems and very dubious benefits, the CTBT should not be ratified.

Despite this division of opinion, the Commission of course recognizes that President Obama has expressed a commitment to "immediately and aggressively" pursue CTBT ratification. In anticipation of Senate review, the Commission wishes to make the following specific recommendations.

*[T]he administration must be able to assure the Senate and the American public that there is an agreed understanding with the other nuclear weapon states about the specific testing activities banned and permitted under the treaty.*

*First*, the Obama administration should help to frame a broad national and international debate about the CTBT by conducting a broad net assessment of the benefits, costs, and risks of ratification and entry into force of the CTBT. The test ban has been a matter of intense, passionate debate for over 50 years and national debate would be very well served by a comprehensive, realistic view of the strengths and weaknesses of the treaty and the trade-offs between them. Especially useful would be an explanation of how such assessments have been shaped by developments since the Senate first considered the treaty.

*Second*, the administration must be able to assure the Senate and the American public that there is an agreed understanding with the other nuclear weapon states about the specific testing activities banned and permitted under the treaty. At present, the United States and Russia (and China) seem to have different interpretations and, if so, this could put the United States at a disadvantage. The treaty itself states that it bans "any nuclear weapon test explosion or other nuclear explosion." Equity must be demonstrated by an agreement of the P-5. An agreed definition of permitted and banned activities must also be verifiable.

*Third*, although U.S. ratification of the CTBT could produce significant diplomatic benefits, it will not bring the treaty into force. Therefore the U.S. should have a credible diplomatic strategy for moving from U.S. ratification to actual entry into force of the treaty and to persuade others not to test. The agreed entry into force provisions of the CTBT dictate that it not enter into force until 44 states have deposited instruments of ratification. In addition to the United States, those states so far not choosing to ratify include

> *[T]he United States must commit to some process of periodic review of the national security consequences of continued adherence to the CTBT, even if not ratified ....*

Egypt, Israel, Iran, India, Pakistan, North Korea, and China. A U.S. decision to proceed with ratification might be influential in motivating some of these states to follow suit, but U.S. ratification alone is unlikely to bring entry into force of the CTBT.

*Fourth*, the United States must commit to some process of periodic review of the national security consequences of continued adherence to the CTBT, even if not ratified, including whether the treaty has entered into force and whether testing is needed to maintain a safe and secure stockpile. The United States must be ready to withdraw from the CTBT and resume testing if the national interest requires.

*Fifth*, the administration and the Congress must demonstrate that they will follow through on the safeguards program. The record of U.S. follow through over the period since signing the CTBT has been mixed. As a general matter, safeguards are a hedge against the risks accepted in arms control treaties. A central risk of the CTBT is that, in the absence of testing, the United States might find it impossible to maintain the safety, security, and reliability of the U.S. nuclear arsenal. As a general matter, safeguards are proposed by the administration and, often after significant discussion, are then included in the Senate resolution providing advice and consent to ratification. In essence, the Senate makes its approval contingent on continued implementation of safeguards, although in practice there is no remedy short of treaty withdrawal if safeguards are not consistently and effectively implemented over the duration of the treaty. Moreover, the safeguards require budgetary support by the House of Representatives which is not involved in the treaty ratification process. There are six such safeguards from 1997, lettered A through F. The CTBT is conditioned on:

A. The conduct of a Science Based Stockpile Stewardship program to insure a high level of confidence in the safety and reliability of nuclear weapons in the active stockpile, including the conduct of a broad range of effective and continuing experimental programs.

B. The maintenance of modern nuclear laboratory facilities and programs in theoretical and exploratory nuclear technology which will attract, retain, and ensure the continued application of our human scientific resources to those programs on which continued progress in nuclear technology depends.

C. The maintenance of the basic capability to resume nuclear test activities prohibited by the CTBT should the United States cease to be bound to adhere to this treaty.

D. Continuation of a comprehensive research and development program to improve our treaty monitoring capabilities and operations.

E. The continuing development of a broad range of intelligence gathering and analytical capabilities and operations to ensure accurate and comprehensive information on worldwide nuclear arsenals, nuclear weapons development programs, and related nuclear programs.

F. The understanding that if the President of the United States is informed by the Secretary of Defense and Secretary of Energy — advised by the Nuclear Weapons Council, the Directors of DOE's nuclear weapons laboratories, and the Commander of the U.S. Strategic Command—that a high level of confidence in the safety or reliability of a nuclear weapon type which the two Secretaries consider to be critical to our nuclear deterrent could no longer be certified, the President, in consultation with Congress, would be prepared to withdraw from the CTBT under the standard "supreme national interests" clause in order to conduct whatever testing might be required.

In the decade since the CTBT was considered by the Senate, there have been some important safeguards successes. In particular, the Stockpile Stewardship Program has had some remarkable achievements. But in recent years, the level of funding provided to support these safeguards has been inadequate. Moreover, as noted in a previous chapter, the Life Extension Program will become increasingly difficult as the stockpile continues to age. Simulations may be helpful in reducing uncertainties but cannot eliminate them. We will need to get back to the funding support that brought about the successes of the Stockpile Stewardship Program.

# Finding

1. The Commission has no agreed position on whether ratification of the CTBT should proceed.

# Recommendations

1. To prepare the way for Senate re-review of the CTBT, the administration should prepare a comprehensive net assessment of benefits, costs, and risks; secure P-5 agreement on a clear and precise definition of banned and permitted test activity; define a diplomatic strategy for entry into force; and prepare a budget that adequately funds the safeguards program.
2. If the Senate consents to CTBT ratification, and acknowledging the expected long delay in actual entry into force of the treaty, the United States should secure agreement among the P-5 to implement CTBT verification provisions without waiting for entry into force of the treaty and to agree to an effective process among the P-5 to permit on-site inspections.

# 10

# On Prevention and Protection

Prior chapters of this report have addressed the challenge of reducing nuclear dangers through a mix of political tools of national policy and an effective deterrent. This chapter highlights some additional steps needed to prevent nuclear proliferation and nuclear terrorism and also to protect the United States and its allies and partners from the consequences of acts not prevented. Three forms of protection are discussed here:

- Counterproliferation measures, principally those focused on interdicting the shipment of weapons or materials to proliferators and terrorists.
- Homeland Defense measures, principally those focused on preventing the transit into the United States of smuggled nuclear weapons or materials.
- Protection against the effects of attack with nuclear weapons designed to have catastrophic electromagnetic pulse (EMP) effects.

Counterproliferation measures emerged as an important adjunct to national nuclear strategy in the 1990s, when it became clear that sometimes nonproliferation efforts would fail and the United States would have to contain and possibly defeat WMD-armed adversaries and to suppress illicit trade among them. Like the Cooperative Threat Reduction program described in a previous chapter, counterproliferation measures were intended to apply new policy tools to new challenges. Over the last decade the counterproliferation effort has burgeoned into a significant international effort under the auspices of the Proliferation Security Initiative (PSI) and similar bilateral and other activities. Sometimes seen as a threat to the nonproliferation regime because they operate outside it, these activities are in fact reinforcing, as they signal the commitment of states to police activities within their territories and in international spaces to ensure that illicit activities are detected and punished. The Commission recommends that such international cooperation to counter proliferation continue.

A parallel activity also merits mention here: the Global Initiative to Combat Nuclear Terrorism. This is a program of activity jointly led by the United States and Russia and aimed at enhancing the capacity of all countries to cope with nuclear terrorism. Partners in this activity share expertise and knowledge about all aspects of countering nuclear terrorism, whether in detecting smuggling, interdicting trade routes, investigating incidents, or treating victims. The Commission recommends that this too continue. The United States has also undertaken significant efforts over the last decade to protect the homeland against nuclear smuggling. This involves improved monitoring of ports where cargo moves in large volume, both in the United States and overseas, and of transportation corridors. Such efforts to protect against nuclear terrorism require strong international cooperation. They also require an improved "whole of government" approach to ensure that the different executive agencies of the U.S. government are engaged in mutually supportive activities. Improved coordination is needed.

> *... efforts to protect against nuclear terrorism require strong international cooperation. They also require an improved "whole of government" approach ....*

These forms of prevention and protection are particularly important to reducing the risks of nuclear terrorism. They are necessary because deterrence seems to have relatively little to contribute to this effort, in contrast to its significant potential impact on state actors. Direct deterrence of terrorists seems impractical with threats of retaliation. After all, terrorists are elusive (and thus they are difficult to target with retaliatory actions) and it has proven difficult to discern what they hold of value or to hold it at risk (and thus they are difficult to restrain through the fear of punishment). To the extent it is practical, deterrence would seem to require an ability to deny terrorists their goals, impede their planning and movement, and attribute the sources of nuclear terrorist attacks. The ability to attribute nuclear terrorist attacks to their sources may also provide some leverage over states whose leaders sponsor terrorism. Policymakers must have a realistic understanding of the difficulties of attribution. Nonetheless, the United States should continue to make efforts to improve the forensic capabilities that can help to evaluate the possible origins of the fissile material in any nuclear detonation.

## The Threat from Electromagnetic Pulse Weapons

Lastly, the United States should take steps to reduce the vulnerability of the nation and the military to attacks with weapons designed to produce electromagnetic pulse (EMP) effects. We make this recommendation although the Commission is divided over how imminent a threat this is. Some commissioners believe it to be a high priority threat, given foreign activities and terrorist intentions. Others see it as a serious potential threat, given the high level of vulnerability. Those vulnerabilities are of many kinds. U.S. power projection forces might be subjected to an EMP attack by an enemy calculating—mistakenly—that such an attack would not involve risks of U.S. nuclear retaliation. The homeland might be attacked by terrorists or even state actors with an eye to crippling the U.S. economy and American society. From a technical perspective, it is possible that such attacks could have catastrophic consequences. For example, successful attacks could shut down the electrical system, disable the internet and computers and the economic activity on which they depend, incapacitate transportation systems (and thus the delivery of food and other goods), etc.

Prior commissions have investigated U.S. vulnerabilities and found little activity under way to address them. Some limited defensive measures have been ordered by the Department of Defense to give some protection to important operational communications. But EMP vulnerabilities have not yet been addressed effectively by the Department of Homeland Security. Doing so could take several years. The EMP commission has recommended numerous measures that would mitigate the damage that might be wrought by an EMP attack. The Stimulus Bill of February 9, 2009, allocates $11 billion to DOE for "for smart grid activities, including to modernize the electric grid." Unless such improvements in the electric grid are focused in part on reducing EMP vulnerabilities, vulnerability might well increase.

## Findings

1. Counterproliferation activities have emerged since the end of the Cold War as a new focus of international cooperation to prevent proliferation and terrorism and they are a useful adjunct to non-proliferation measures.
2. Stronger "whole of government" approaches are needed to reduce the risks of nuclear smuggling into the United States.
3. The United States is highly vulnerable to attack with weapons designed to produce electromagnetic pulse effects.

## Recommendations

1. The Proliferation Security Initiative and Global Initiative to Combat Nuclear Terrorism should be sustained and additional international

cooperative measures developed to prevent and protect against proliferation and terrorism.

2. Improved integration of national and international responses is needed to protect the homeland against nuclear smuggling. The U.S. government should accelerate the development of sensors to detect nuclear smuggling and deploy them when effective.

3. EMP vulnerabilities should be reduced as the United States modernizes its electric power grid.

# 11

# Closing Observations

As the Commission has debated its findings and recommendations, it has become clear that we have very different visions of what might be possible in the long term. Fundamentally, this reflects our differences over whether the conditions can ever be created that might enable the elimination of nuclear weapons. But our debates have also brought home to us that we share, to a very significant degree, a vision of the nearer term.

Looking ahead over the next decade or two, we reject the notion that somehow it is inevitable that international nuclear order will collapse. Despite the many challenges in the international security environment, there is no reason to accept as inevitable the collapse of the nonproliferation regime, a cascade of proliferation to new states, an associated dramatic rise in the risks of nuclear terrorism, and a return of competition for nuclear advantage among the major powers.

On the contrary—the past successes of the United States and its international partners in meeting and reducing nuclear dangers make us more hopeful for the future. We embrace the possibility that over the next decade or two nuclear dangers will be further reduced. The risks of nuclear terrorism can be reduced through stronger cooperative measures to control their access to materials, technology, and expertise. The major powers can cooperate more effectively in service of nonproliferation, strategic stability among themselves, and steadily diminishing reliance on nuclear weapons. While the United States may not be able to prevent all proliferation, there may be some rollback of current programs and capabilities and also continued restraint by most. The United States and its allies and friends can be made to feel more secure and the pressures on others to seek nuclear weapons diminished.

> *[T]he past successes of the United States and its international partners in meeting and reducing nuclear dangers make us more hopeful for the future.*

Despite our many differences of opinion, we have come together around a strategy that offers pragmatic steps for bringing this vision closer to reality. It is firmly grounded in the strategic tradition of the United States and the twin imperatives to meet nuclear dangers with effective deterrence and to reduce them where possible with additional political means, including principally arms control and nonproliferation.

Many of us see one component of strategy as more important than the other. But none of us would endorse a strategy that emphasizes one approach to the near exclusion of the other. These two components of strategy should be mutually reinforcing. Extended deterrence, for example, reinforces non-proliferation, by assuring U.S. allies and friends that they need not create independent nuclear deterrents of their own to be secure. Conversely, non-proliferation regimes help create the political conditions to allow enforce-ment actions against dangerous states.

Of course, in any comprehensive strategy policies associated with one component might sometimes conflict with those associated with the other. Such potential conflicts must be recognized and, where possible, resolved so that the components of policy can be brought into balance. If the United States puts too much or too little emphasis on nuclear weapons, this could undermine arms control and nonproliferation. If it pursues an arms control strategy that reduces needed nuclear forces unilaterally, this could under-mine deterrence and assurance, in turn undermining nonproliferation. Bal-ance is needed and we believe that our recommendations strike the needed balance.

While so heavy an emphasis on nuclear deterrence is not needed today, an awareness of its critical role needs to be restored in the United States and this too must be emphasized by our national leaders. We have delineated a strategy for deterrence that ensures a strong and effective deterrent so long as it is needed, but we have aligned our recommendations with the need for balance through changes to declaratory policy and force structure. We have also delineated a strategy for arms control and nonproliferation that promises to significantly reduce nuclear dangers, but this too has been aligned with the need for balance through the commitment to maintaining a safe, secure, and reliable stockpile of nuclear weapons. We rec-ognize that critics on both sides of this debate will find fault with the compromises we have proposed. But a lop-sided approach will not im-prove U.S. security and a balanced approach to reducing nuclear dangers is essential.

*In surveying more than six decades of nuclear history, we are struck by the fact that nuclear weapons have not been used since 1945. It is clear that a tradition against the use of nuclear weapons has taken hold.*

In surveying more than six decades of nuclear history, we are struck by the fact that nuclear weapons have not been used since 1945. It is clear that a tradition against the use of nuclear weapons has taken hold. The United States must strive to maintain this tradition and urge all other nuclear armed nations to adhere to it. At the end of World War II, the United States tried to establish an international authority to restrict nuclear technology exclusively to peaceful purposes, called the Baruch plan; however, the plan failed. Since very few nuclear weapons existed at that time, this concept might have succeeded had the Soviet Union been ruled by a Gorbachev and not by Stalin. Yet the tradition of non-use has now lasted more than six decades. In at least four wars a nuclear-armed power accepted defeat or stalemate fighting an enemy that did not have a single nuclear bomb: the Korean war, the U.S. war in Vietnam, the Soviet Union's war in Afghanistan, and China's cross-border attack on Vietnam.

Any future use of nuclear weapons is likely to be the beginning of a catastrophic change in the world order. Those nations able to strengthen their nuclear forces, or to start to acquire nuclear weapons of their own, would likely do so. Thus, nuclear proliferation would be accelerated, and the 63-year-old dividing line between conventional and nuclear could be erased. To survive in such a violent world would be particularly difficult for democracies. It would change the world order in fundamental ways and would risk a highly unstable nuclear disorder. Dictatorship might benefit from the worldwide nuclear violence. Clearly, preserving this tradition of non-use is essential.

# Compilation of Findings and Recommendations

## Chapter One: On Challenges and Opportunities

### Findings

1. Throughout the nuclear era U.S. policy has been shaped by the imperative to reduce nuclear dangers with a balanced approach involving both deterrence and political measures such as arms control and nonproliferation. Although evolving circumstances over the six decades of the nuclear era have compelled leaders to innovate and adapt, there has been striking continuity in U.S. strategic policy.

2. Since the end of the Cold War, the nuclear security environment of the United States has changed considerably. The threat of a nuclear Armageddon has largely disappeared. But new threats have taken shape and the overall environment has grown more complex and in some ways more precarious.

3. The U.S. strategic posture and doctrine have also changed substantially in the intervening period. The U.S. nuclear force is but a small fraction of what it was at the end of the Cold War and the U.S. reliance on nuclear weapons in national military strategy and national security strategy has been sharply reduced.

4. Nuclear terrorism against the United States and other nations is a very serious threat. This requires a much more concerted international response, one which the United States must lead.

5. Nuclear and missile proliferation could have a profoundly negative impact on the global security environment. The further uncontrolled diffusion of nuclear materials, technology, and expertise would likely accelerate the future rate of proliferation. It would certainly increase the risks of nuclear terrorism.

6. The opportunities to further engage Russia as a partner in reducing nuclear dangers are important and should be seized. The United States must also continue to concern itself with issues of deterrence, assurance, and stability in the nuclear relationship with Russia.

7.  The opportunities to engage China are also significant. But here too the United States must balance deterrence and stability concerns with the opportunities for strategic cooperation.
8.  These developments in major power nuclear relations and proliferation affect U.S. allies and friends at least as much as they affect the United States. Their particular views of the requirements of extended deterrence and assurance in an evolving security environment must be understood and addressed by the United States.
9.  The conditions that might make the elimination of nuclear weapons possible are not present today and establishing such conditions would require a fundamental transformation of the world political order. Nonetheless, the Commission recommends a number of steps that can reduce nuclear dangers.
10. For the indefinite future, the United States must maintain a viable nuclear deterrent. The other NPT-recognized nuclear-weapon states have put in place comprehensive programs to modernize their forces to meet new international circumstances.
11. The executive and the Congress need to renew dialogue on these issues.

## Recommendations

1.  The United States should continue to pursue an approach to reducing nuclear dangers that balances deterrence, arms control, and nonproliferation. Singular emphasis on one or another element would reduce the nuclear security of the United States and its allies.
2.  The United States must retain nuclear weapons until such time as the international environment may permit their elimination globally.
3.  To address the serious risk of nuclear terrorism, the United States needs strong intelligence and reenergized international cooperation through its deterrence, nonproliferation, and arms control efforts. The best defense against nuclear terrorism is to keep nuclear bombs and fissile material out of the hands of terrorists.
4.  The United States should adapt its strategic posture to the evolving requirements of deterrence, extended deterrence, and assurance. As part of an effort to understand assurance requirements, steps to increase allied consultations should be expanded.
5.  The United States should reverse the decline of focus and resources of the Intelligence Community devoted to foreign nuclear weapons capabilities, programs, and intentions. With some important exceptions, this subject has not attracted high-level attention since

the end of the Cold War. As will be discussed later, the weapons laboratories have an important role to play here.

6. The practice and spirit of executive-legislative dialogue on nuclear strategy that helped pave the way for bipartisanship and continuity in policy should be renewed. The Senate should revive the Arms Control Observer Group.

# Chapter Two: On the Nuclear Posture

## Findings

1. The U.S. nuclear posture consists of many elements, including operationally deployed strategic nuclear weapons; forward-deployed tactical nuclear weapons; the triad of strategic nuclear delivery systems; the delivery systems for forward-deployed weapons; the stockpile of warheads held in operational reserve; a stockpile of fissile material appropriate for use in warheads; the associated command, control, and intelligence systems; and the infrastructure associated with the production of all of these capabilities.

2. There is no right number of weapons needed for the U.S. strategic posture other than one that is derived from a complex decision-making process, originating with the president. To determine that number, the strategic context must be assessed. Political judgment from the highest level of the government is required. Numbers associated with different force sizes must be set in a strategic context.

3. In formulating an overall posture, the United States should employ a broad concept of deterrence. Extended deterrence and dissuasion and the need to hedge against uncertainty have design implications for the posture.

4. The sizing of U.S. forces remains overwhelmingly driven by Russia. For the deterrence of attacks by regional powers or terrorists, the weapons requirements are relatively modest. Even deterrence of China does not require large numbers. Currently, no one seriously contemplates a direct Russian attack on the United States. Some U.S. allies located closer to Russia are fearful of Russia and look to the United States for reassurance.

5. The United States could maintain its security while reducing its reliance on nuclear weapons and making further reductions in the size of its stockpile, if this were done while also preserving the resilience and survivability of U.S. forces. Substantial stockpile reductions would need to be done bilaterally with the Rus-

sians, and at some level of reductions, with other nuclear powers. But some potential reductions in non-deployed weapons need not await Russia. The United States could reduce its reliance on, and thus supply of, reserve warheads if it were to refurbish the nuclear infrastructure.

## Recommendations

1. The force structure should be sized (and shaped) to meet a diverse set of national objectives. This requires a high-level assessment of strategic context. Reductions in deployed forces should be made on the basis of bilateral agreement with Russia.
2. Deterrence considerations, broadly defined, should inform the development of the next U.S. strategic posture.
3. The triad of strategic delivery systems continues to have value. Each leg of the nuclear triad provides unique contributions to stability. As the overall force shrinks, their unique values become more prominent.
4. The United States should also retain capabilities for the delivery of non-strategic nuclear weapons and proceed in close consultation with allies in Europe and Asia in doing so.
5. Force posture design and arms control should keep stability and U.S. credibility as their central objectives.
6. Steps should be taken to ensure the continued viability of the infrastructure supporting delivery systems.

# Chapter Three: On Missile Defense

## Findings

1. Missile defenses effective against regional nuclear aggressors, including against limited long-range threats, are a valuable component of the U.S. strategic posture.

## Recommendations

1. The United States should develop and, where appropriate, deploy missile defenses against regional nuclear aggressors, including against limited long-range threats. It should also develop effective capabilities to defend against increasingly complex missile threats.
2. While the missile threats posed by potential regional aggressors are countered, the United States should ensure that its actions do

not lead Russia or China to take actions that increase the threat to the United States and its allies and friends.

3. The United States should strengthen international cooperation for missile defense, including with allies, but also with Russia.

4. The United States should also work with Russia and China to control advanced missile technology transfer.

# Chapter Four: On Declaratory Policy

## Finding

1. Effective deterrence and assurance requires that U.S. declaratory policy be understood to reflect the intentions of national leadership.

## Recommendations

1. The United States should reaffirm that the purpose of its nuclear force is deterrence, as broadly defined to include also assurance of its allies and dissuasion of potential adversaries.

2. It should not abandon calculated ambiguity by adopting a policy of no-first-use.

3. The United States should make clear that it conceives of and prepares for the employment of nuclear weapons only in extreme circumstances.

4. The United States should reiterate its commitments to NPT parties as stated in the agreed positive and negative security assurances, as they were qualified by both the Clinton and Bush administrations.

# Chapter Five: On the Nuclear Weapons Stockpile

## Findings

1. The United States requires a stockpile of nuclear weapons that is safe, secure, and reliable, and whose threatened use in military conflict would be credible.

2. The reliability of existing warheads is reviewed for certification on an annual basis by the directors of the nuclear weapons laboratories. Maintaining the reliability of the warheads as they age is an increasing challenge.

3. The Life Extension Program has to date been effective in dealing with the problem of modernizing the arsenal. But it is becoming

increasingly difficult to continue within the constraints of a rigid adherence to original materials and design as the stockpile continues to age.

4. Alternatives to this approach exist and involve, to varying degrees, the reuse and/or redesign of components and different engineering solutions.

5. The debate over the Reliable Replacement Warhead revealed a lot of confusion about what was intended, what is needed, and what constitutes "new."

6. So long as modernization proceeds within the framework of existing U.S. policy, it should encounter the minimum political difficulty. As a matter of U.S. policy, the United States does not produce fissile materials and does not conduct nuclear explosive tests. Also, the United States does not currently seek new weapons with new military characteristics. Within this framework, it should seek the possible benefits of improved safety, security, and reliability available to it.

## Recommendations

1. The decision on which approach to refurbishing and modernizing the nuclear stockpile is best should be made on a type-by-type basis as the existing stockpile of warheads ages.

2. The Commission recommends that Congress authorize the NNSA to conduct a cost and feasibility study of incorporating enhanced safety, security, and reliability features in the second half of the planned W76 life extension program. This authorization should permit the design of specific components, including both pits and secondaries, as appropriate.

3. Similar design work in support of the life extension of the B61 should be considered if appropriate, as well as for other warheads as they come due for modernization.

4. Red-teaming should be used to ensure an intellectually competitive process that results in a stockpile of weapons meeting the highest standards of safety, security, and reliability.

5. The Significant Findings Investigations flowing from on-going surveillance of the stockpile should be utilized by leadership, including in the Congress, to monitor the technical health of the stockpile.

6. The United States maintains an unneeded degree of secrecy with regard to the number of nuclear weapons in its arsenal (including not just deployed weapons but also weapons in the inactive stockpile and those awaiting dismantlement). Secrecy policies should be

reviewed with an eye toward providing appropriate public disclosure of stockpile information.

# Chapter Six: On the Nuclear Weapons Complex

## Findings

1. The physical infrastructure is in serious need of transformation. The National Nuclear Security Administration (NNSA) has a reasonable plan for doing so that should be reviewed seriously by the Congress. But it lacks the needed funding.

2. Once the plutonium pit production facility at Los Alamos (TA55/PF-4) is fully operational, it should be sufficient for expected U.S. needs.

3. The intellectual infrastructure is also in serious trouble. A major cause is the recent (and projected) decline in resources. A significant additional factor is the excessively bureaucratic management approach of NNSA, which is antithetical to effective research and development.

4. Attracting and retaining the top national talent and expertise requires that the laboratories conduct challenging research on important national problems. This program of work must be sustained and predictable and exercise the full range of laboratory skills, including nuclear weapon design skills. Exercising these design skills is necessary to maintain design and production engineering capabilities. Skills that are not exercised will atrophy.

5. Elements of the federal government outside DOE are keen to utilize the capabilities of the weapons laboratories but they are not keen to invest in the underlying science and engineering that generates those capabilities.

6. The relationship between the laboratories and the intelligence community merits particular attention, given its importance and sensitivity. Some recent budgetary decisions have significantly weakened their collaboration.

7. The governance structure of the NNSA is not delivering the needed results. Despite some success, NNSA has failed to meet the hopes of its founders. It lacks the needed autonomy. This structure should be changed.

8. NNSA's problems will not vanish simply by implementing a new reporting structure. The regulatory burden on the laboratories is excessive and should be rationalized.

9.  NNSA needs the resources to perform its assigned missions. Although the NNSA decision to modernize in place is the right decision, the budget risk appears extremely high. The hope that consolidation would save money is unwarranted. Other important laboratory activities may pay a significant price. To juggle all of its competing commitments NNSA would have to reduce its base of scientific activity by 20-30 percent even in a flat budget and this would have a significant impact on the science and engineering base. NNSA does not know how large the core laboratory weapons programs need to be to maintain the deterrent.

10. Future infrastructure requirements must be assessed in light of the results of arms control negotiations now underway. Depending on progress in U.S.-Russian arms reductions, some downsizing may be possible.

## Recommendations

1.  Congress should reject the application of the BRAC concept to NNSA. There would be no cost savings and no other efficiencies. Congress should fund the NNSA complex transformation plan while also ensuring that the needed scientific and engineering base is maintained. The plan will not be realized without a one-time infusion of funding above current spending levels and this should be done.

2.  If complex transformation must proceed without such an infusion, either complex transformation will be significantly delayed or the intellectual infrastructure will be seriously damaged. If the two major proposed construction projects must be prioritized, give priority to the Los Alamos plutonium facility. In a flat or declining budget scenario, strong oversight must ensure that schedule and workforce issues are balanced in a way that does not substantially cripple current enterprise capabilities.

3.  As part of the effort to protect the scientific and engineering basis, NNSA should adopt a management approach consistent with the requirements of the effectiveness of research and development organizations. A less bureaucratic approach is required. Useful reforms include a realignment of DOE, NNSA, NRC, and DNFSB roles and responsibilities as elaborated in the text of the chapter.

4.  The Congress should fund the test readiness program in order to maintain the national policy of readiness to test within 24 months.

5.  NNSA should conduct a study of the core competencies needed in the weapons complex, and the Congress and Office of Management

and Budget should use these as a tool for determining how to fund NNSA.

6. The President should designate the nuclear weapons laboratories as National Security Laboratories. This would recognize the fact that they already contribute to the missions of the Departments of Defense and Homeland Security and the intelligence community in addition to those of DOE. The president should assign formal responsibility to the Secretaries of Energy, Defense, State, and Homeland Security and the Director of National Intelligence for the programmatic and budgetary health of the laboratories.

7. Congress should amend the NNSA Act to establish NNSA as a separate agency reporting to the President though the Secretary of Energy. The legislation should include the additional specific provisions identified in this chapter.

8. The Director of National Intelligence should review and assess the potential contributions of the laboratories to the national intelligence mission and advocate for the needed allocation of resources. Congress should provide sustained support.

9. Congress and the Administration should also create a formal mechanism (not involving awarding fee) to recognize the importance of the involvement of the directors of the weapons laboratories in the annual certification process.

10. NNSA should adopt a more coherent approach to security that utilizes tools such as conditional probability metrics to set standards and that creates incentives that are as responsive to success as they are to failure.

# Chapter Seven: On Arms Control

## Findings

1. Arms control should and can play an important role in reducing nuclear dangers.

2. In both Washington and Moscow, the moment appears ripe to renew the arms control process.

3. The imbalance of non-strategic nuclear weapons will become more prominent and worrisome as strategic reductions continue and will require new arms control approaches that are also assuring to U.S. allies.

4. For the United States to reduce its deployed nuclear forces, it is essential to move by agreement with Russia.

## Recommendations

1. Pursue a step-by-step approach with Russia on arms control. This is a process that will play out over years and decades.
2. Make the first step on U.S.-Russian arms control modest and straightforward in order to rejuvenate the process and ensure that there is a successor to the START I agreement before it expires at the end of 2009. The United States and Russia should not over-reach for innovative approaches.
3. Begin to characterize and study the numerous challenges that would come with any further reductions in the number of operationally deployed strategic nuclear weapons.
4. Sustain the commitment to the INF treaty and commit to new efforts to work in partnership with Russia and NATO allies to negotiate reductions in non-strategic nuclear forces.
5. Develop and pursue options for advancing U.S. interests in stability in outer space and in increasing warning and decision-time. The options should include the possibility of negotiated measures.
6. Take the lead in renewing strategic dialogue with a broad set of states interested in strategic stability, including not just Russia and China but also U.S. allies in both Europe and Asia.
7. Work to come to an understanding with Moscow on missile defense, if possible. The United States should explore more fully Russian concerns. The two should define measures that can help build needed confidence. Pursue possible technical and operational collaboration in this area where mutually beneficial. Revive the moribund effort to establish a joint warning center.
8. Reinvest in the institutional capacities needed to define and implement effective arms control strategies. The pattern of underinvestment over the last two decades must be reversed.

# Chapter Eight: On Nonproliferation

## Findings

1. This is an opportune moment to reenergize nonproliferation. Both domestic and international conditions are favorable.
2. Despite the occasional failure of nonproliferation, the historical track record is good and we hope to find continued success in the years ahead. But the stakes are rising and we may be on the brink of a

new cascade of proliferation. This underscores the urgency of acting now.

3. Success in advancing U.S. nonproliferation interests requires U.S.
   leadership. Leadership requires leading by example.

4. Growing reliance on nuclear energy will bring with it a sharp rise
   in the number of facilities using and producing fissile materials, a
   much broader trade in the associated technologies, and a further
   globalization of nuclear expertise. This will inevitably increase the
   risks of possible diversion to illicit purposes.

## Recommendations

1. Renew multifaceted diplomatic activity and engagement.

2. Strengthen the International Atomic Energy Agency. Stronger financial, technical, and political support for the IAEA by the United
   States and from its Board of Governors could enhance its ability to
   perform its unique and important mission.

3. Working in partnership with Russia, the United States should lead
   a global initiative on transparency, addressing both warheads and
   stockpiles.

4. Seek a treaty that ends the production of fissile material for weapons
   purposes and pursue verification provisions that enable its effective
   implementation.

5. Augment funding for threat reduction activities that strengthen
   controls at vulnerable nuclear sites.

6. Develop international approaches to future nuclear energy production that minimize proliferation risks.

7. Prepare to play a leadership role at the 2010 NPT review conference.

8. Publicize more effectively the steps the United States has already
   taken to meet its Article VI commitments.

# Chapter Nine: On the CTBT

## Finding

1. The Commission has no agreed position on whether ratification of
   the CTBT should proceed.

## Recommendations

1. To prepare the way for Senate re-review of the CTBT, the administration should prepare a comprehensive net assessment of benefits, costs, and risks; secure P-5 agreement on a clear and precise definition of banned and permitted test activity; define a diplomatic strategy for entry into force; and prepare a budget that adequately funds the safeguards program.
2. If the Senate consents to CTBT ratification, and acknowledging the expected long delay in actual entry into force of the treaty, the United States should secure agreement among the P-5 to implement CTBT verification provisions without waiting for entry into force of the treaty, and also to have more effective means to get on-site inspections.

# Chapter Ten: On Prevention and Protection

## Findings

1. Counterproliferation activities have emerged since the end of the Cold War as a new focus of international cooperation to prevent proliferation and terrorism and they are a useful adjunct to nonproliferation measures.
2. Stronger "whole of government" approaches are needed to reduce the risks of nuclear smuggling into the United States.
3. The United States is highly vulnerable to attack with weapons designed to produce electromagnetic pulse effects.

## Recommendations

1. The Proliferation Security Initiative and Global Initiative to Combat Nuclear Terrorism should be sustained and additional international cooperative measures developed to prevent and protect against proliferation and terrorism.
2. Improved integration of national and international responses is needed to protect the homeland against nuclear smuggling. The U.S. government should accelerate the development of sensors to detect nuclear smuggling and deploy them when effective.
3. EMP vulnerabilities should be reduced as the United States modernizes its electric power grid.

# Appendix 1

# Glossary

| | |
|---|---|
| **AEC** | Atomic Energy Commission |
| **BRAC** | Base Realignment and Closure Commission |
| **CMRR** | Chemistry and Metallurgy Research Replacement |
| **CTBT** | Comprehensive Test Ban Treaty |
| **DNFSB** | Defense Nuclear Facilities Safety Board |
| **DoD** | Department of Defense |
| **DOE** | Department of Energy |
| **EMP** | electromagnetic pulse |
| **EU** | European Union |
| **FERC** | Federal Energy Regulatory Commission |
| **FMCT** | Fissile Material Cut-off Treaty |
| **GAO** | Government Accountability Office |
| **IAEA** | International Atomic Energy Agency |
| **ICBM** | intercontinental ballistic missile |
| **IG** | inspector general |
| **INF** | Intermediate-range Nuclear Forces Treaty |
| **NATO** | North Atlantic Treaty Organization |
| **NNSA** | National Nuclear Security Administration |

**NPR** Nuclear Posture Review

**NPT** Non-Proliferation Treaty

**NRC** Nuclear Regulatory Commission

**NSNF** non-strategic nuclear forces

**OMB** Office of Management and Budget

**OSHA** Occupational Safety and Health Administration

**P-5** United Nations Security Council permanent members

**PAC-3** Patriot Advanced Capability-3

**PNI** Presidential Nuclear Initiatives

**PSI** Proliferation Security Initiative

**R&D** research and development

**RRW** Reliable Replacement Warhead

**SFI** Significant Findings Investigation

**SLBM** submarine-launched ballistic missile

**SORT** Strategic Offensive Reductions Treaty

**START** Strategic Arms Reductions Treaty

**THAAD** Terminal High Altitude Area Defense

**TLAM/N** Tomahawk Land Attack Missile/Nuclear

**UNSCR** United Nations Security Council Resolution

**UPF** Uranium Processing Facility

**WMD** weapons of mass destruction

# Appendix 2

# Estimated World Nuclear Warhead Arsenals[a]

## Estimated Nuclear Warhead Inventories

|                                       | U.S.          | Russia              |
|---------------------------------------|---------------|---------------------|
| **Peak number of weapons (year)**     | 32,000 (1967) | 40,000 (USSR; 1986) |
| **Current weapons (total)**           | 9,400         | 13,000              |
| *Strategic operational*               | 4,700         | 4,100               |
| *Non-strategic operational*           | < 500         | 3,800               |
| *Reserve and awaiting dismantlement*  | 4,200         | 5,100               |

*The United States has reduced its warhead total by about a factor of four since the end of the Cold War, and Russia has reduced by almost a factor of four.*

—National Nuclear Security Administration
   March 16, 2009

## Other Nuclear Countries Today

| Country        | Number of Weapons |
|----------------|-------------------|
| China          | 400               |
| France         | 300               |
| United Kingdom | < 200             |
| Israel         | 100-200           |
| India          | 50-60             |
| Pakistan       | 60                |
| North Korea    | "a few," <10      |

Sources: Nuclear Threat Initiative; Dr. Sig Hecker; Federation of American Scientists

(a): note that more precise numbers are generally classified; these numbers, particularly for Russia, Israel, India, Pakistan, and North Korea, should be considered as approximate.

# Enabling Legislation and Joint Explanatory Statements

## National Defense Authorization Act for FY 2008
### (P.L. 110-181)

### SEC. 1062. CONGRESSIONAL COMMISSION ON THE STRATEGIC POSTURE OF THE UNITED STATES.

(a) ESTABLISHMENT.—There is hereby established a commission to be known as the "Congressional Commission on the Strategic Posture of the United States". The purpose of the commission is to examine and make recommendations with respect to the long-term strategic posture of the United States.

(b) COMPOSITION.—

  (1) MEMBERSHIP.—The commission shall be composed of 12 members appointed as follows:

   (A) Three by the chairman of the Committee on Armed Services of the House of Representatives.

   (B) Three by the ranking minority member of the Committee on Armed Services of the House of Representatives.

   (C) Three by the chairman of the Committee on Armed Services of the Senate.

   (D) Three by the ranking minority member of the Committee on Armed Services of the Senate.

  (2) CHAIRMAN; VICE CHAIRMAN.—

   (A) CHAIRMAN.—The chairman of the Committee on Armed Services of the House of Representatives and the chairman of the Committee on Armed Services of the Senate shall jointly designate one member of the commission to serve as chairman of the commission.

   (B) VICE CHAIRMAN.—The ranking minority member of the Committee on Armed Services of the House of Representatives and the ranking minority member of the Committee on Armed Services of the Senate shall jointly designate one member of the commission to serve as vice chairman of the commission.

(3) **PERIOD OF APPOINTMENT; VACANCIES.**—Members shall be appointed for the life of the commission. Any vacancy in the commission shall be filled in the same manner as the original appointment.

**(c) DUTIES.**—

(1) **REVIEW.**—The commission shall conduct a review of the strategic posture of the United States, including a strategic threat assessment and a detailed review of nuclear weapons policy, strategy, and force structure.

(2) **ASSESSMENT AND RECOMMENDATIONS.**—

(A) ASSESSMENT.—The commission shall assess the benefits and risks associated with the current strategic posture and nuclear weapons policies of the United States.

(B) RECOMMENDATIONS.—The commission shall make recommendations as to the most appropriate strategic posture and most effective nuclear weapons strategy.

**(d) COOPERATION FROM GOVERNMENT.**—

(1) **COOPERATION.**—In carrying out its duties, the commission shall receive the full and timely cooperation of the Secretary of Defense, the Secretary of Energy, the Secretary of State, the Director of National Intelligence, and any other United States Government official in providing the commission with analyses, briefings, and other information necessary for the fulfillment of its responsibilities.

(2) **LIAISON.**—The Secretary of Defense, the Secretary of Energy, the Secretary of State, and the Director of National Intelligence shall each designate at least one officer or employee of the Department of Defense, the Department of Energy, the Department of State, and the intelligence community, respectively, to serve as a liaison officer between the department (or the intelligence community, as the case may be) and the commission.

**(e) REPORT.**—Not later than December 1, 2008, the commission shall submit to the President, the Secretary of Defense, the Secretary of Energy, the Secretary of State, the Committee on Armed Services of the Senate, and the Committee on Armed Services of the House of Representatives a report on the commission's findings, conclusions, and recommendations. The report shall identify the strategic posture and nuclear weapons strategy recommended under subsection (c)(2)(B) and shall include—

(1) the military capabilities and force structure necessary to support the strategy, including both nuclear and non-nuclear capabilities that might support the strategy;

    (2) the number of nuclear weapons required to support the strategy, including the number of replacement warheads required, if any;

    (3) the appropriate qualitative analysis, including force-on-force exchange modeling, to calculate the effectiveness of the strategy under various scenarios;

    (4) the nuclear infrastructure (that is, the size of the nuclear complex) required to support the strategy;

    (5) an assessment of the role of missile defenses in the strategy;

    (6) an assessment of the role of nonproliferation programs in the strategy;

    (7) the political and military implications of the strategy for the United States and its allies; and

    (8) any other information or recommendations relating to the strategy (or to the strategic posture) that the commission considers appropriate.

(f) **FUNDING.**—Of the amounts appropriated or otherwise made available pursuant to this Act to the Department of Defense, $5,000,000 is available to fund the activities of the commission.

(g) **TERMINATION.**— The commission shall terminate on June 1, 2009.

# Joint Explanatory Statement to accompany the National Defense Authorization Act for Fiscal Year 2008

## Congressional commission on the strategic posture of the United States (sec. 1062)

The House bill contained a provision (sec. 1046) that would establish a 12 member congressional commission on the strategic posture of the United States to examine and make recommendations with respect to the long-term strategic posture of the United States. The review and assessment to be conducted by the commission would include a threat assessment, a detailed review of nuclear weapons policy and strategy of the United States, and recommendations as to the most appropriate strategic posture and most effective nuclear weapons strategy. The commission's report would be due to Congress and the Executive Branch no later than December 1, 2008. The term of the commission would expire on June 1, 2009. In addition, the provision would repeal section 1051 of the National Defense Authorization Act for Fiscal Year 2006 (Public Law 109–163).

The Senate amendment contained no similar provision.

The Senate recedes with an amendment that would clarify that the vice chairman of the commission would be jointly appointed by the ranking minority members of the Committees on Armed Services of the House of Representatives and the Senate. In addition, the amendment would clarify that the commission should look at non-nuclear alternatives to nuclear weapons and systems in making recommendations with respect to the most appropriate strategic posture and most effective nuclear weapons policies of the United States.

The conferees urge the commission to look at the strategic posture of the United States in the broadest sense. Strategic policy and posture is not synonymous with nuclear policy. Conventional force structures, as well as nuclear force structures, must be included in the overall review and assessment of the strategic posture of the United States.

In addition, the conferees believe that many of the nuclear missions of the United States could be served by non-nuclear, conventional systems. In their examination of the strategic posture of the United States, the conferees expect the commission to look not only at nuclear capabilities, but at the full array of non-nuclear capabilities, including kinetic and non-kinetic capabilities.

The conferees have included a separate provision addressing the repeal of section 1051 of the National Defense Authorization Act for Fiscal Year 2006 elsewhere in this Act.

# National Defense Authorization Act for FY 2009
## (P.L. 110-417)

### SEC. 1060. EXTENSION OF CERTAIN DATES FOR CONGRESSIONAL COMMISSION ON THE STRATEGIC POSTURE OF THE UNITED STATES.

(a) **EXTENSION OF DATES.**—Section 1062 of the National Defense Authorization Act for Fiscal Year 2008 (Public Law 110–181) is amended— (1) in subsection (e), by striking "December 1, 2008" and inserting "April 1, 2009"; and (2) in subsection (g), by striking "June 1, 2009" and inserting "September 30, 2009".

(b) **INTERIM REPORT.**—Not later than December 1, 2008, the Congressional Commission on the Strategic Posture of the United States shall submit to the President, the Secretary of Defense, the Secretary of Energy, the Secretary of State, the Committee on Armed Services of the Senate, and the Committee on Armed Services of the House of Representatives an interim report on the commission's initial findings, conclusions, and recommendations. To the extent practicable, the interim report shall address the matters required to be included in the report under subsection (e) of such section 1062.

## Joint Explanatory Statement to accompany the National Defense Authorization Act for Fiscal Year 2009

### Extension of certain dates for Congressional Commission on the Strategic Posture of the United States (sec. 1060)

The House bill contained a provision (sec. 1032) that would extend the due date for the final report of the Congressional Commission on the Strategic Posture of the United States from December 1, 2008 to March 1, 2009, and the sunset date for the Commission from June 1, 2009, to September 30, 2009. The provision would also direct the Commission to submit an interim report no later than December 1, 2009. The Senate bill contained no similar provision. The agreement includes the House provision with an amendment that that would extend the due date of the final report to April 1, 2009. The Commission should be prepared to brief Congress on the results of the interim report when it becomes available.

## National Defense Authorization Act for FY 2009 (P.L. 110-417)

### SEC. 1060. EXTENSION OF CERTAIN DATES FOR CONGRESSIONAL COMMISSION ON THE STRATEGIC POSTURE OF THE UNITED STATES.

(a) **EXTENSION OF DATES.**—Section 1062 of the National Defense Authorization Act for Fiscal Year 2008 (Public Law 110–181) is amended— (1) in subsection (e), by striking "December 1, 2008" and inserting "April 1, 2009"; and (2) in subsection (g), by striking "June 1, 2009" and inserting "September 30, 2009".

(b) **INTERIM REPORT.**—Not later than December 1, 2008, the Congressional Commission on the Strategic Posture of the United States shall submit to the President, the Secretary of Defense, the Secretary of Energy, the Secretary of State, the Committee on Armed Services of the Senate, and the Committee on Armed Services of the House of Representatives an interim report on the commission's initial findings, conclusions, and recommendations. To the extent practicable, the interim report shall address the matters required to be included in the report under subsection (e) of such section 1062.

# Interim Report of the Congressional Commission on the Strategic Posture of the United States

### December 11, 2008

## 1. Charge to the Commission and Interim Activities

Pursuant to the responsibilities assigned to it in the FY08 National Defense Authorization Act, the Congressional Commission on the Strategic Posture of the United States began its work in spring 2008. A delay in securing funding for the commission meant that the first commission meeting occurred in July. Accordingly, and by agreement with the Congressional sponsors of the legislation, delivery of the Commissioni's final report has been postponed from December 1, 2008 until April 1, 2009. This document serves as the requested interim report on the work of the Commission to date.

The Commission was chartered to provide findings, conclusions, and recommendations. At this time it would be premature to offer recommendations. Rather, our purpose with this interim report is to review briefly the progress of our efforts and to offer interim findings on some of the relevant issues.

The Commission has convened approximately monthly to hear the views of others with information and expertise germane to our task.

Our first priority was to meet with interested members of the Congress, and we have heard from various individuals from both houses and both parties. From these meetings, we took many away several important messages. Perhaps the most important was the Congressional desire to better understand the key ideas on which a sufficient measure of political consensus can be built to enable effective long-term implementation of national strategy.

We have also met with administration representatives to gain a better understanding of its policies and programs and of the key concepts underpinning them. From the Department of Defense, we have learned about the halting efforts to implement the 2001 Nuclear Posture Review and the more recent effort to make a joint cabinet-level statement on nuclear policy. From the National Nuclear Security Administration and the nuclear laboratories we have learned about the efforts to create an enhanced Stockpile Stewardship Program and to adapt to evolving planning and programming requirements. In general, we have gained an improved appreciation of the efforts of the current leadership of the US nuclear enterprise, who are working under the difficult circumstances of a lack of national consensus. Both the DOD and NNSA have been fully cooperative and exceptionally helpful.

We have also devoted considerable time and energy to interacting with representatives of foreign governments interested in the outcome of this effort and also of the next US Nuclear Posture Review. We have gained important new insights into the perspectives of US allies on the requirements of extended deterrence and assurance and also of the expectations of many other states for US leadership.

To study the many questions of policy and strategy within the Commissionís purview, we formed five working groups of experts drawn from across the political spectrum. They are exploring issues of strategic policy and strategy, force structure and deterrence, countering proliferation, infrastructure, and the evolving security environment. We tasked these groups with specific questions, but also asked them to bring issues before us they deem important. This has helped to deepen and broaden our understanding of key issues.

We have had timely and substantive assistance from the cognizant federal agencies, including the intelligence community, among others.

In conducting our work, we have adopted a broad definition of the strategic posture. We are looking not just at the traditional issues within the purview of a Nuclear Posture Review, such as the size and shape of the nuclear force and its associated roles and missions. Rather, we defined the scope of our work to include all uses of nuclear weapons and all tools to counter the nuclear threat, including for example missile defense and countering nuclear proliferation. But we also defined some limits to our inquiry. For example, we have chosen not to expand our scope of work to encompass the problems associated with all weapons of mass destruction, though we have included in our review the question of whether and how nuclear weapons have a role in deterring attacks with chemical and biological weapons.

We are also taking a broad view of the elements of strategy by looking beyond the military domain. The legislation poses a series of broad questions about US strategy and how the tools of policy can be integrated to achieve US objectives. We are looking broadly at political, economic, and military tools, and expect to craft a report that addresses all three. We note, however, that the legislation clearly puts emphasis on the military tools and especially nuclear questions. We understand that the lack of consensus about the future of the US nuclear deterrent is a key motivator of the charge to the Commission.

As we continue our work, we welcome further interaction with interested members of Congress. We look forward to submission of our report on April 1 and the ensuing dialogue about needed improvements to the US strategic posture.

## 2. Dealing with the Changing Strategic Challenge

During the Cold War the Soviet Union posed an existential threat to the United States. In response to this threat, successive presidents consistently increased the effectiveness of our nuclear weapon systems, with deployments of more than 10,000 nuclear warheads in American strategic forces by 1980. With the dissolution of the Soviet Union and the ending of the Cold War, the danger of an existential threat dramatically decreased. This has permitted the United States to reduce its reliance on nuclear weapons and substantially reduce our nuclear forces. The current superiority of US conventional capabilities has reinforced this process. (Ironically, our edge in conventional capabilities has induced the Russians, now feeling their conventional deficiencies, to increase their reliance on both tactical and strategic nuclear weapons.)

Although the existential threat to the United States has dramatically decreased, the fact that other states possess nuclear weapons continues to affect decisions about the needed US strategic posture. The size of our nuclear deterrent continues to be driven in part by the size of Russian nuclear forcesóas well as Russiaís doctrinal embrace of greater reliance on tactical as well as strategic nuclear weapons. China in this connection remains a lesser consideration. Proliferation is also an important factor, not least for the demands it places on a credible US extended deterrent.

As the existential threat has waned, a new threat has come to the foreóthat of catastrophic terrorism. 9-11 demonstrated all too clearly that Al Qaeda and other terror groups wished to inflict mass casualties on Americans. And we know that Al Qaeda has sought nuclear weapons to achieve that end. But a terror group cannot make a nuclear bomb from scratch, so the best defense against this threat is to prevent terror groups from acquiring a nuclear bomb or the fissile material from which they could perhaps make a bomb.

Achieving that defense leads to four security imperatives:

- To reduce and provide better protection for existing nuclear stockpiles of weapons and fissile material;
- To keep new nations from going nuclear;

- To provide effective protection for the fissile material generated by enrichment activities, reprocessing facilities, and commercial nuclear reactors; and
- To improve our tools to detect clandestine delivery of nuclear weapons and to disable and otherwise defend against them.

None of these imperatives can be achieved unilaterally. We can reduce and protect our own stockpiles, but we need cooperation from other nations, especially Russia, to be sure that their stockpiles do not leak to terror groups. Since the early 90s we have worked cooperatively with Russia in the reduction and protection of stockpiles, but today cooperation with Russia is increasingly in question because of the generally strained geopolitical relations between the United States and Russia.

The efforts to keep other nations from going nuclear are obviously multinational. The 6-party talks have had limited success to date in dealing with North Korea but may ultimately be successful. However, there is no similarly comprehensive diplomatic approach to Iran, which has constructed a major facility for enriching uranium.

It appears that we are at a "tipping point" in proliferation. If Iran and North Korea proceed unchecked to build nuclear arsenals, there is a serious possibility of a cascade of proliferation following. And as each new nuclear power is added the probability of a terror group getting a nuclear bomb increases.

Even if a terror group is not able to acquire a weapon from a nuclear state, it could build a crude nuclear device if it were able to acquire the necessary fissile material. The International Atomic Energy Agency (IAEA) has proposed strengthening the Nuclear Non-Proliferation Treaty (NPT) safeguards to provide far better protection of fissile material, but to date is not getting the needed support for its proposals.

Thus dealing with the increasingly dangerous threat of proliferation requires us to find a way of cooperating with many other nations, including, but not limited to, all of the nuclear powers. And it requires working effectively with the IAEA. What we do in our own nuclear weapon program has a significant effect on (but does not guarantee) our ability to get that cooperation. In particular, this cooperation will be affected by what we do in our weapons laboratories, what we do in our deployed nuclear forces, what kind of nuclear policies we articulate, and what we do regarding arms control treaties (e.g., START and CTBT). It is not clear that actions we take on our nuclear program affect the nuclear calculus of North Korea or Iran, or necessarily others, but they do affect the actions of nations whose cooperation we need to deal with North Korea and Iran, as well as other proliferation problems. In short, if the US by its actions indicates to other nations that we are moving seriously to decrease the importance and role of nuclear weapons, we increase our chance of getting the kind of cooperation we need to deal effectively with the dangers of proliferation.

But some actions that might promote cooperation could be in conflict with the actions needed to maintain the reliability, safety and security of our nuclear forces. So, as long as we need to maintain such forces, our challenge is to define a nuclear program that contributes to decreasing the global dangers of proliferation, including maintaining the needed reliability, safety and security of our nuclear weapons and maintaining the role they play in overall stability and the reassurance of allies. Given the uncertainties in the factors affecting global security today, the need for deterrence (and extended deterrence) could extend for an indefinite future.

Since the ending of the Cold War, we have embarked on a number of critical programs to enhance the reliability, safety and security of our nuclear stockpile. Specifically, the Stockpile Stewardship Program was initiated at our nuclear labs in the early 1990s. This program has engaged some of the best scientists and best scientific facilities in the world and has been remarkably successful. The Stockpile Stewardship Program (SSP), as originally intended, has provided greater confidence in our nuclear weapons without explosive testing. But support for this program is at risk and needs to be renewedóas our weapons get older they require continuing fiscal and political support. The SSP was established in part to give the US confidence in the reliability of the stockpile and thus to renounce nuclear testingóand sign the CTBT. Maintaining a robust SSP would be a prerequisite for ratification of the treaty.

Critical to maintaining confidence in our stockpile is the Life Extension Program, which assesses the capability of existing warheads and makes component modifications as needed to maintain their capability. As we get farther from the date those weapons were designed, this program becomes more difficult to execute. A few years ago the administration proposed to deal with this problem by designing new warheads, which it called Reliable Replacement Warheads (RRW). After a lengthy debate, Congress did not authorize the development of RRW but did authorize work on Advanced Certification. In considering future life extension programs, DoD and NNSA are exploring opportunities to make more significant changes in the weapons than has occurred in previous refurbishment programs. These changes include "mining" existing components from non-deployed weapons to assure long-term reliability and increased safety and security of weapons kept in the force. Also fundamental to the continuing effectiveness of the stockpile is the long-term stability of plutonium, which was unknown at the time of the signing of the CTBT. In the last few years, scientists at the labs and a group of university scientists (JASON) have concluded that the plutonium pits in our stockpile will remain viable for 85 years or longer.

High confidence in stockpile reliability not only is important for maintaining deterrence, it is also vital for making substantial reductions in the size of our stockpile. In particular, high confidence in the reliability of the stockpile could allow us to consider giving up thousands of weapons we keep in reserve. And for the same reason, it could allow us to enter into negotiations with Russia to make further reductions in the number of deployed nuclear weapons, reserve weapons, and nuclear delivery systems.

So the political environment has changed in fundamental ways since the Cold War, calling for a new assessment of the role nuclear weapons should play in our security. The security of the US no longer depends on maintaining the large number of nuclear weapons needed during the Cold War. Indeed, major reductions already have been made in the American and Russian nuclear stockpiles. Both the US and Russia believe, however, that their security will depend on maintaining a deterrence force of some size for the foreseeable future. As long as that is true, it will be necessary for the US to maintain the reliability, security and safety of the residual nuclear force; the smaller the size of the stockpile, the more important it will be to have confidence in its reliability.

As the political environment has changed, so also has our technological understanding of nuclear weapons advanced, allowing us to maintain confidence in our stockpile even as our weapons age. But those technological advances have resulted from extraordinary achievements by the scientists of our weapons labs under a well-funded SSP and Life Extension Program. And they have depended on human capital that is in increasingly short supply. Sustaining support for those scientists and those programs is a prerequisite to maintaining continuing confidence in the reliability of the stockpile. And the smaller the stockpile becomes, the more important it will be to sustain the labsí scientific expertise.

## 3. Some Interim Findings

The Commission continues to gather information for analysis with the intention of identifying relevant findings and crafting recommendations that will be contained in the final report. That said, we have noted several findings that are consistent with the information gathered to date:

Nuclear terrorism poses a growing nuclear threat to the nation. The best defense against such terrorism is keeping the nuclear bombs and fissile material out of the hands of terror groups. Such a non-proliferation strategy, to be effective, would require intense cooperation with other nations, especially other nuclear powers, and with the IAEA.

The proliferation threat is also growing. Unless the Iranian program is halted short of a weapons capability and the North Korean program reversed and its arsenal dismantled, there is likely to be a proliferation cascade that would greatly increase the risks of nuclear use and terrorism.

Although Russia and China do not pose a nuclear threat to the US, they do have an extensive nuclear capability that could do grievous damage to us (as we to them). Given uncertainty about their political direction and international roles, the United States cannot afford to ignore the requirements of deterrence.

While the Nation should continue to commit to reducing its reliance on nuclear weapons and act transparently on that commitment, the US must also continue to maintain a nuclear deterrent *appropriate to existing threats* until such time as verifiable international agreements are in place that could set the conditions for the final abolition of nuclear and other weapons of mass destruction. As long as the US depends on nuclear deterrence, national policies must ensure that this deterrence is reliable, safe and secure.

Effective deterrence (and assurance) requires clear declaratory policy from the United States. To be effective, such policy must be understood to reflect the intentions of national leadership.

Deterrence of non-state actors is much more problematic. To the extent it is practical, it would seem to require an ability to attribute the sources of nuclear terrorist attacks. The US must have a realistic understanding of the difficulties of attribution. But it should also continue to make efforts to improve the forensic capabilities that can help to evaluate the possible origins of the fissile material in any nuclear detonation.

Our non-proliferation strategy will continue to depend upon US *extended deterrence strategy* as one of its pillars. Our military capabilities, both nuclear and conventional, underwrite US security guarantees to our allies, without which many of them would feel enormous pressures to create their own nuclear arsenals. So long as the United States maintains adequately strong conventional forces, it does not necessarily need to rely on nuclear weapons to deter the threat of a major conventional attack. But long-term US superiority in the conventional military domain cannot be taken for granted and requires continuing attention and investment. Moreover, it is not adequate for deterring nuclear attack. The US deterrent must be both visible and credible, not only to our possible adversaries, but to our allies as well.

Four senior statesmen have urged that the nation work towards the global elimination of nuclear weapons. It is clear that the goal of zero nuclear weapons is extremely difficult to attain and would require a fundamental transformation of the world political order. If, however, the new administration accepts their proposal as a long-term goal, there are steps that could be taken in the next few years that would be consistent with such a goal and, at the same time, consistent with maintaining and even increasing our security. Some of our recommendations will deal with such steps.

The US could maintain its security while reducing its reliance on nuclear weapons and making further reductions in the size of its stockpile, if this is done appropriately. Substantial stockpile reductions would need to be done bilaterally with the Russians, and at some level of reductions, with other nuclear powers. But some types of reductions need not await Russia, especially if the US nuclear infrastructure is refurbished, allowing the US to reduce its reliance on and supply of reserve warheads.

There is little likelihood of other nations eliminating their nuclear arsenals just because the United States does so. Potential proliferant nations may be drawn to consider acquiring nuclear capabilities not because of US nuclear strength, but as a way for them to address our substantial conventional force superiority to which they can feel vulnerable. Such nations believe their nuclear weapons serve as their "equalizer."

The threat of nuclear terrorism is strongly reinforced by any proliferation and the possibility that nuclear weapons might deliberately be passed on to terrorists or stolen by them.

The Stockpile Stewardship Program has been a remarkable success, much more than originally expected. However, the program may be in danger of losing the support needed to adequately fund it.

Although the Life Extension Program has been successful to date, it will face increasing challenges as components age and more changes are made. In our final report we intend to define the most efficient and effective way to maintain a credible, safe, secure, and reliable deterrent for the long term. We recognize also that broader infrastructure issues must be addressed in any such program.

The NPT has long provided the essential legal framework for preventing proliferation. But it is not sufficient for this purpose—and was never intended to be. It must be supplemented with other tools of policy. Its effectiveness has been undermined by errors in how it has been interpreted and by failures of enforcement by the UN Security Council. The 2010 Review Conference provides an opportunity to renew international efforts to address these problems with the legal framework. The US ought to begin now to set the stage by engaging with friends and allies on those issues related to desired improvements.

While the International Atomic Energy Agency (IAEA) may not always act as we would wish, it continues to play an indispensable role and to support critical US interests. Stronger financial, technical, and political support for the IAEA by the United States could enhance its ability to perform its unique and important mission.

Missile defenses appropriate to defend against a rogue nuclear nation could serve a damage-limiting and stabilizing role in the US strategic posture, assuming such defenses are perceived as being effective enough to at least sow doubts in the minds of potential attackers that such an attack would succeed. On the other hand, levels of defenses sizable enough to sow such doubts in the minds of Russia or China could lead them to take actions that increase the threat to the US and its allies and friends.

The advent of a new administration creates the opportunity to open a new strategic dialogue with Russia. One objective of this dialogue could be a new arms treaty that provides for further significant reductions in the nuclear arsenals of the two countries. The Commission is prepared strongly to endorse negotiations with Russia in order to proceed jointly to further reductions in our nuclear forces, as part of a cooperative effort to stabilize relations, stop proliferation, and promote predictability and transparency. The large Russian arsenal of tactical nuclear weapons must be considered in this regard. However, any negotiated reduction between Russia and the US should not be carried out in a manner that might incentivize the Chinese to undertake a program to increase their nuclear capabilities in an effort to compete with us.

The United States has not conducted an explosive nuclear test since 1992. Since that time the SSP, through the use of analytical simulation, laboratory experiments, and the Life Extension Programs, has maintained the stockpile without nuclear testing. The new administration may consider resubmitting the CTBT to the Senate for ratification. A negotiated agreement defining and banning such testing could offer important benefits compared to an informal moratorium. Before submission the DOE and DoD should receive from the labs and STRATCOM clear statements describing the future capabilities and flexibility required to minimize the risks of maintaining a credible, safe, and reliable nuclear deterrent without nuclear explosive testing.

The Department of Energy's laboratory system provides invaluable support to the nation in three ways. First, it actively maintains the safety, security, reliability and effectiveness of the stockpile over the long term. Second, the system is the wellspring of the talent and tools needed to address a multitude of national problems, such as nonproliferation research, nuclear threat reduction, nuclear forensics, bioterrorism defense, missile defense, countering improvised explosive devices, nuclear energy, and alternative energy options. Finally, the system plays an important role in maintaining the intellectual scientific leadership of the United States.

## 4. Next Steps

The Commission recognizes that its mandate covers several other issues. Defining an appropriate strategic posture requires our developing a concept of "strategic posture" from which will devolve force structure and arsenal requirements. However, in keeping with the intent of Congress to broaden the scope of our work beyond the traditional focus on nuclear strategy and weapons, we will develop the relationship between our force structure/capabilities and both our arms control and non-proliferation strategies. The combination of these three will produce for Congress a workable construct of ìstrategic posture.î The final report will contain our analysis, findings, conclusions and recommendations related to this concept.

To that end, the Commission will undertake the following:

- Conduct a qualitative analysis of our national capabilities with emphasis on maintaining a strategic posture appropriate to the requirements of contemporary national goals such as deterrence and assurance (including nuclear force structure and delivery systems, etc.) and on countering proliferation and countering nuclear terrorism.
- Examine the current state of arms control and how to integrate it with the other two broad components of strategic posture. Consideration will be given to potential new objectives for re-engaging Russia in a strategic dialogue.
- Study the development of an integrated nonproliferation strategy combining regional and global diplomatic initiatives closely coupled to unilateral policies and programs.
- Continue an assessment of the nuclear complex infrastructure through on-site visits.
- Address the importance of the six-decade-long record of non-use of nuclear weapons and the danger for the world order if this pattern were broken. We will explore the importance for the US and all nations of maintaining this de facto moratoriumó and the means of doing so.

# Commission Plenary Sessions Schedule

May 19, 2008 (Commission Organization meeting)

June 17, 2008 (First full plenary meeting)

July 14-15, 2008

September 16, 2008 (Congressional meetings on Capitol Hill)

September 29-30, 2008 (Trip to Lawrence Livermore National Laboratory)

October 8-9, 2008

November 7, 2008

December 1-2, 2008

January 7-9, 2009 (Plenary and trip to Oak Ridge, TN)

February 24-25, 2009

March 16-17, 2009

April 1-2, 2009

# Appendix 6

# Consultations

## Members of Congress

### United States Senate

Senator Jeff Sessions (R-AL) *Ranking Member, Armed Services Committee Sub-Committee on Strategic Forces*

Senator Jon Kyl (R-AZ) *Minority Whip*

Senator Bill Nelson (D-FL) *Chairman, Armed Services Committee Sub-Committee on Strategic Forces*

### United States House of Representatives

Representative Ellen O. Tauscher (D-CA) Chairman, *Armed Services Committee Sub-Committee on Strategic Forces*

Representative Terry Everett (R-AL) *Ranking Member, Armed Services Committee Sub-Committee on Strategic Forces*

Representative Duncan Hunter (R-CA) *Ranking Member, Armed Services Committee*

Representative Peter Visclosky (D-IN) *Chairman, Appropriations Committee Sub-Committee on Energy and Water*

Representative Peter Hoekstra (R-MI) *Ranking Member, Permanent Select Committee on Intelligence*

Representative David Hobson (R-OH) *Ranking Member, Appropriations Committee Sub-Committee on Energy and Water*

Representative Silvestre Reyes (D-TX) *Chairman, Permanent Select Committee on Intelligence*

# Current U.S. Administration Officials

## Department of State

John Rood—*Under Secretary of State for Arms Control and International Security*

## Department of Defense/Military

*Civilian:*

Robert Gates—*Secretary of Defense*

Fred Celic—*Deputy Assistant to the Secretary of Defense (Nuclear Matters)*

Michael O. Wheeler—*Director, Advanced Systems and Concepts Office, DTRA*

S. Steve Henry—*Director, Office of Nuclear Matters*

David J. Stein—*Director, Office of Strategic Strike Options*

*Military:*

General James E. Cartwright—*Vice Chairman of the Joint Chiefs of Staff*

General Kevin P. Chilton—*Commander, U.S. Strategic Command*

Lieutenant General Patrick J. O'Reilly—*Director, Missile Defense Agency*

## Department of Energy

Samuel W. Bodman—*Secretary of Energy (2005-2009)*

Thomas D'Agostino—*Administrator, National Nuclear Security Administrator*

George H. Miller—*Director, Lawrence Livermore National Laboratory*

Michael R. Anastasio—*Director, Los Alamos National Laboratory*

Thomas O. Hunter—*Director, Sandia National Laboratories*

Daniel P. Kohlhorst—*President and General Manager, Y-12 National Security Complex*

Theodore Sherry—*Manager, Y-12 Site Office*

Greg Meyer—*General Manager, B&W Pantex Plant*

Chris Gentile—*Vice President, Savannah River Site*

Carl Beard—*Associate Director, Los Alamos National Laboratory*

Bob Jensen—*Vice President, Kansas City Plant*

## Director of National Intelligence
John M. McConnell—*Director of National Intelligence (2007-2009)*

# Arms Control Groups

David Albright—*Institute for Science and International Security*

Jack Mendelsohn—*Arms Control Association*

John Issacs—*Council for a Livable World*

Ivan Oelrich—*Federation of American Scientists*

David Culp—*Friends Committee on National Legislation*

Christopher Paine—*Natural Resources Defense Council*

Stephen Young—*Union of Concerned Scientists*

James Leonard—*British American Security Information Council*

Jeffrey Lewis—*New America Foundation*

Jeff Kueter—*The Marshall Institute*

Baker Spring—*The Heritage Foundation*

Daniel Goure—*The Lexington Institute*

Sam Nunn—*Nuclear Threat Initiative*

Joan Rohlfing—*Nuclear Threat Initiative*

Ilan Berman—*American Foreign Policy Council*

Peter Huessy—*National Defense University Foundation*

# Foreign Officials

Takeo Akiba—*Minister, Head of Political Section, Embassy of Japan (2009)*

Masafumi Ishii—*Minister, Head of Political Section, Embassy of Japan (2008)*

Hidetoshi Iijima—*First Secretary, Political Section, Embassy of Japan*

Masaaki Kanai—*First Secretary, Political Section, Embassy of Japan*

Friis Arne Petersen—*Ambassador, Embassy of Denmark*

Nabi Sensoy—*Ambassador, Embassy of the Republic of Turkey*

Ihsan Kiziltan—*Counselor, Embassy of the Republic of Turkey*

Klaus Scharioth—*Ambassador, Embassy of the Federal Republic of Germany*

Hans-Peter Hinrichsen—*Counselor, Embassy of the Federal Republic of Germany*

Jacques Audibert—*Director for Strategic Affairs, International Security and Disarmament, Ministry of Foreign Affairs, France*

Martin Briens—*Deputy Director for Nuclear Nonproliferation and Disarmament, Ministry of Foreign Affairs, France*

Nicolas Roche—*Counselor, Embassy of France*

Sallai Meridor—*Ambassador, Embassy of Israel*

Amir Maimon—*Minister Counselor, Embassy of Israel*

Wegger Chr. Strommen—*Ambassador, The Royal Norwegian Embassy*

Odd-Inge Kvalheim—*Minister Counsellor, The Royal Norwegian Embassy*

Lee Tae-sik—*Ambassador, Embassy of the Republic of Korea*

Hyoung Z. Kim—*Minister Counselor, Embassy of the Republic of Korea*

Chang-ho Yoo—*First Secretary, Embassy of the Republic of Korea*

Sergey I. Kislyak—*Ambassador of the Russian Federation to the United States*

Vassily V. Boriak—*Senior Counselor, Embassy of the Russian Federation*

Dennis Richardson—*Ambassador, Embassy of Australia*

Peter Sawczak—*Political Counsellor, Embassy of Australia*

Celia Perkins—*Defence Counsellor, Embassy of Australia*

Scott Furssedonn—*First Secretary, Strategic Threats, British Embassy*

Clare Bloomfield—*Foreign and Security Policy Office, British Embassy*

## Other Experts

Richard Garwin—*IBM Fellow Emeritus, Thomas J. Watson Research Center*

Michael Quinlan—*International Institute for Strategic Studies (deceased)*

# Appendix 7

# Expert Working Groups

## National Security Strategy and Policies

**Ashton Carter** (Chairman), Harvard University (Resigned Jan. 2009)

**James Miller** (Chairman), Center for a New American Strategy

**Elbridge Colby,** RAND Corporation

**J.D. Crouch,** National Institute for Public Policy

**James F. Dobbins,** RAND Corporation

**William Fallon,** Massachusetts Institute of Technology

**Michele A. Flournoy,** Center for a New American Strategy (Resigned Jan. 2009)

**Andy Krepinevich,** Center for Strategic and Budgetary Assessments

**Richard Mies,** Admiral, U.S. Navy (Ret.)

**Steve Rosen,** Harvard University

**William Schneider,** Defense Science Board

**Elizabeth Sherwood-Randall,** Stanford University (Resigned Jan. 2009)

**Philip D. Zelikow,** University of Virginia

## Deterrent Force Posture

**Dennis C. Blair** (Chairman), National Bureau of Asian Research (Resigned Jan. 2009)

**Thomas Scheber** (Chairman), National Institute for Public Policy

**Barry Blechman,** Henry L. Stimson Center

**Elaine Bunn,** National Defense University

**John Hillen,** Global Strategies Group, LLC

**Ronald F. Lehman,** Lawrence Livermore National Laboratory

**Frank Miller,** The Cohen Group

**Clark Murdock,** Center for Strategic and International Studies

**Janne E. Nolan,** Georgetown University and University of Pittsburgh

**Harold Palmer Smith, Jr.,** University of California, Berkeley

## Nuclear Infrastructure

**Linton Brooks** (Chairman), former NNSA Administrator

**Robert Barker,** Lawrence Livermore National Laboratory (Retired)

**Everett Beckner,** Consultant

**Henry Chiles,** Admiral, U.S. Navy (Retired)

**Steve Guidice,** Independent Consultant

**John Gordon,** General, U.S. Air Force (Retired)

**Burgess Laird,** Institute for Defense Analyses

**Ernest Moniz,** Massachusetts Institute of Technology

**C. Paul Robinson,** Sandia National Laboratory (Retired)

**Harold Smith,** University of California, Berkeley

**Troy Wade,** Former Assistant Secretary of Energy for Defense Programs

**Earl Whiteman,** National Nuclear Security Administration (Retired)

## Countering Proliferation

**Arnold Kanter** (Chairman), The Scowcroft Group

**Daniel Poneman** (Vice Chairman), The Scowcroft Group

**Kathleen C. Bailey,** National Institute for Public Policy

**Joseph Cirincione,** Ploughshares Fund

**Lewis A. Dunn,** Science Applications International Corporation

**Robert Einhorn,** Center for Strategic and International Studies

**James E. Goodby,** Stanford University

**Siegfried Hecker,** Stanford University

**Rebecca Hersman,** National Defense University

**Susan Koch,** U.S. Department of State

**Mitchell Reiss,** William and Mary School of Law

**Scott Sagan,** Stanford University

**Henry Sokolski,** Nonproliferation Policy Education Center

## External Conditions and Trends

**Gordon Oehler** (Chairman), The Potomac Institute for Policy Studies

**Richard Kerr,** MITRE Corporation

**John McLaughlin,** Johns Hopkins University

**Joseph Nye,** Harvard University

**Michelle Van Cleve,** National Defense University

# Appendix 8

# Commissioner Biographies

## William J. Perry—*Chairman*

William Perry is the Michael and Barbara Berberian Professor at Stanford University, with a joint appointment at the Freeman Spogli Institute (FSI) and the School of Engineering. He is a senior fellow at FSI and serves as co-director of the Preventive Defense Project, a research collaboration of Stanford and Harvard Universities.

He is an expert in U.S. foreign policy, national security and arms control. He was the co-director of Center for International Security and Cooperation from 1988 to 1993, during which time he was also a professor (half time) at Stanford. He was a part-time lecturer in the Department of Mathematics at Santa Clara University from 1971 to 1977.

Perry was the 19th Secretary of Defense for the United States, serving from February 1994 to January 1997. He previously served as deputy secretary of defense (1993-1994) and as under secretary of defense for research and engineering (1977-1981). He is on the board of directors of LGS Bell Labs Innovations and several emerging high-tech companies and is chairman of Global Technology Partners.

His previous business experience includes serving as a laboratory director for General Telephone and Electronics (1954-1964); founder and president of ESL Inc. (1964-1977); executive vice-president of Hambrecht & Quist Inc. (1981-1985); and founder and chairman of Technology Strategies & Alliances (1985-1993). He is a member of the National Academy of Engineering and a fellow of the American Academy of Arts and Sciences.

From 1946 to 1947, Perry was an enlisted soldier in the Army Corps of Engineers, and served in the Army of Occupation in Japan. He joined the Reserve Officer Training Corps in 1948 and was a second lieutenant in the Army Reserves from 1950 to 1955. He has received a number of awards, including the Presidential Medal of Freedom (1997), the Department of Defense Distinguished Service Medal (1980 and 1981), and Outstanding Civilian Service Medals from the Army (1962 and 1997), the Air Force (1997), the Navy (1997), the Defense Intelligence Agency (1977 and 1997), NASA (1981) and the Coast Guard (1997). He received the American Electronic Association's Medal of Achievement (1980), the Eisenhower Award (1996), the Marshall Award

(1997), the Forrestal Medal (1994), and the Henry Stimson Medal (1994). The National Academy of Engineering selected him for the Arthur Bueche Medal in 1996. He has received awards from the enlisted personnel of the Army, Navy, and the Air Force.

He has received decorations from the governments of Albania, Bahrain, France, Germany, Hungary, Japan, Korea, Poland, Slovenia, Ukraine, and the United Kingdom. He received a BS and MS from Stanford University and a PhD from Penn State, all in mathematics.

## James R. Schlesinger—*Vice Chairman*

James R. Schlesinger currently divides his time between MITRE, where he serves as Chairman of the Board, and the investment banking firm of Barclays Capital, where he serves as senior advisor. He is also a consultant to the Departments of Defense and State, and a member of the Defense Policy Board and the International Security Advisory Board.

Schlesinger is a fellow of the National Academy of Public Administration and a member of the American Academy of Diplomacy. He is a director for Evergreen Energy and Sandia National Corporation. He is also a counselor and trustee of the Center for Strategic and International Studies (CSIS), a trustee at the Atlantic Council, the Nixon Center, the National Cryptologic Museum Foundation, the Center for Global Energy Studies, and the Henry M. Jackson Foundation.

Schlesinger was the nation's first secretary of energy, taking the oath of office one day after President Carter signed the legislation creating the new department. He served in this position from August 5, 1977 until 1979. In the previous year, President-elect Carter had asked Schlesinger to become assistant to the president, charged with the responsibility of drafting a plan for the establishment of the Department of Energy and a national energy policy.

From July 1973 to November 1975 Schlesinger was secretary of defense. Immediately prior to this appointment, he served as director of central intelligence. In August 1971 he was selected by President Nixon to become chairman of the Atomic Energy Commission, a position he held until February 1973.

Schlesinger began his government service in 1969 as assistant director of the U.S. Bureau of the Budget (later the Office of Management and Budget), where he also served as acting deputy director.

He was a senior staff member at the RAND Corporation from 1963 to 1967, and RAND's director of strategic studies from 1967 to 1969. He also served as consultant to the Board of Governors of the Federal Reserve System and to the Bureau of the Budget.

From 1955 to 1963 he was assistant and then associate professor of economics at the University of Virginia.

Schlesinger has also served on many government commissions and advisory groups. Recently, he served as Chairman of the Secretary's Task Force on DoD Nuclear Weapons Management. He is also Vice Chairman of the Congressional Commission on the Strategic Posture of the United States. From 1999 to 2003 he was a member of the Panel to Assess the Reliability, Safety, and Security of the U.S. Nuclear Stockpile, and from 1998 to 2001 he was a member of the U.S. Commission on National Security/21st Century (Hart-Rudman Commission). He recently served as co-chair of Defense Science Board Task Force on the Future of the Global Positioning System. He also served on an independent team reviewing the Global Positioning System for the U.S. Air Force. He was vice chairman of the President's Blue Ribbon Task Group on Nuclear Weapons Program Management (1984–1985), and served on the Governor's Commission on Virginia's Future (1982–1984) and the President's Commission on Strategic Forces (1982–1983).

Schlesinger has been awarded eleven honorary doctorates. He is the recipient of the National Security Medal, as well as five departmental and agency medals. He is the recipient of the Dwight D. Eisenhower Distinguished Service Medal, the George Catlett Marshall Medal, the H. H. Arnold Award, the Navy League's National Meritorious Citation, the Distinguished Service Award of the Military Order of the Carabao, the Jimmy Doolittle Award, the Military Order of the World Wars Distinguished Service Award, the Henry M. Jackson Award for Distinguished Public Service, and the William Oliver Baker Award.

Schlesinger is the author of *The Political Economy of National Security*, 1960, *America at Century's End*, 1989, and numerous articles.

In 1950 Schlesinger received a bachelor of arts degree *summa cum laude* from Harvard College, where he was elected to Phi Beta Kappa and was selected for the Frederick Sheldon Prize Fellowship. He received his master of arts and doctoral degrees from Harvard University in 1952 and 1956, respectively.

## Harry E. Cartland—*Member*

Harry Cartland is an independent technical consultant and entrepreneur in such areas as defense, space launch, and renewable energy. Most recently, Cartland served as a senior member of the personal staff for Congressman Duncan Hunter. In this capacity, he managed defense and border security related issues for California's 52nd District and the Ranking Member of the House Committee on Armed Services. From June 2005 to January 2007, Cartland was a senior member of the professional staff for the House Committee on Armed Services. During this time he led a special oversight team for the full committee chairman as well as managed the staff of the Projection Forces Subcommittee.

From July 2004 to May 2005, Cartland was as an independent consultant on technical projects and public policy issues, particularly in the area of missile defense. For three years, starting in June 2001 Cartland served as a member of the professional staff of the House Committee on Armed Services, managing the staff of the Subcommittee on Strategic Forces after its establishment in 2003. He contributed technical expertise to the committee staff across a wide range of national security issues.

Beginning in April 1993, Cartland served as project leader and physicist for Lawrence Livermore National Laboratory in Livermore, CA. He worked as a special projects leader for the engineering department at Livermore and organized a response to congressional inquiry regarding the National Laboratories' capabilities to assist the Department of Defense with their theater and national missile defense programs.

From September 1992 until March 1993, Cartland was a visiting scholar at Duke University in the physics department and a consultant at the US Army Research Office in North Carolina. In this capacity, he provided technical advice to the ARO, including in the emerging area of nanotechnology. Cartland had previously served on active duty in the US Army, with assignments to the faculty of the United States Military Academy and the staff of the US Army Ballistic Research Laboratory.

Cartland has published scientific articles and papers on a range of topics, including in the Journal of Physical Chemistry, the Journal of Applied Physics, Chemical Physics Letters, and the Johns Hopkins APL Technical Digest.

Cartland has received a number of awards and distinctions over the years, including the Walter G. Berl Award from Johns Hopkins University APL (1999), and the Scientific Achievement Medallion at the Army Science Conference (1992, 1990), and was a distinguished graduate of the US Army Chemical School (1991, 1985). He is a member of the American Physical Society, the American Chemical Society and the American Association for the Advancement of Science.

Born in Fort Knox, Kentucky in 1958, Cartland graduated with a BA in Chemistry from Cornell University in 1980, where he was elected to Phi Beta Kappa. In 1985, Cartland completed his PhD in Physical Chemistry at the University of California, Berkeley.

# John S. Foster—*Member*

John S. Foster, Jr. is Chairman of the Board of GKN Aerospace Transparency Systems, Co-Chairman Nuclear Strategy Forum, member of the board of Wackenhut Services, Inc., and consultant to Northrop Grumman Corp., Sikorsky Aircraft Corp., Intellectual Ventures, and Defense Group Inc.

He retired from TRW as Vice President, Science & Technology, in 1988 and continued to serve on the Board of Directors of TRW from 1988 to 1994.

Foster began his career at the Radio Research Laboratory of Harvard University in 1942. He spent 1943 and 1944 as an advisor to the 15th Air Force on radar and radar countermeasures in the Mediterranean Theater of Operations, and the summers of 1946 and 1947 with the National Research Council of Chalk River, Ontario.

In 1952, Foster participated in the start-up of the Lawrence Livermore Laboratory and designed nuclear explosives. He became a division leader at the laboratory and he was promoted to Associate Director in 1958, and served as Director of the Livermore Laboratory and Associate Director of the Lawrence Berkeley National Laboratory from 1961 to 1965.

Foster was Director of Defense Research and Engineering for the Department of Defense, serving for eight years (1965–1973) under both Democratic and Republican administrations.

Foster served on the Air Force Scientific Advisory Board until 1956. He then served on the Army Scientific Advisory Panel until 1958 and was a member of the Ballistic Missile Defense Advisory Committee, Advanced Research Projects Agency in 1965. He has served on and off as a panel consultant to the President's Science Advisory Committee. From 1973 until 1990, he was a member of the President's Foreign Intelligence Advisory Board. He is a Senior Fellow member of the Defense Science Board and served as Chairman of the DSB from January 1990 to June 1993. He currently serves on the Congressional Commission on the Strategic Posture of the United States and on the Advisory Committee to the Director of DARPA.

Foster was born September 18, 1922 in New Haven, Connecticut. He received his bachelor's of science degree from McGill University, Montreal, in 1948. He received his doctorate in physics from the University of California, Berkeley in 1952.

Among his numerous honors are the Department of Defense Eugene Fubini Award (1998), the Founders Award from the National Academy of Engineering (1989) and the 1992 Enrico Fermi Award. In 1979 he received an honorary Doctor of Science from the University of Missouri. Other awards include: The Ernest Orlando Lawrence Memorial Award of the Atomic Energy Commission (1960), the Defense Department's Distinguished Public Service Medals (1969, 1973, 1993), election of the National Academy of Engineering

(1969), the James Forrestal Memorial Award (1969), the HH Arnold Trophy (1971), the Crowell Medal (1972), the WEMA Award (1973) and the Knight Commander's Cross (Badge and Star) of the Order of Merit of the Federal Republic of Germany (1974). Foster is a commander, Legion of Honor, Republic of France.

He is a member of the American Defense Preparedness Association, National Advisory Board of the American Security Council, National Security Industrial Association and the American Institute of Aeronautics and Astronautics.

## John Glenn—*Member*

John H. Glenn was born on July 18, 1921, in Cambridge, Ohio. During his early childhood, the family moved to New Concord, Ohio, where Glenn attended primary and secondary school. Following graduation from New Concord High School, Glenn enrolled in Muskingum College and began flying lessons at the New Philadelphia airport, earning his pilot's license in 1941. Following Pearl Harbor, he left college and enlisted in the Naval Aviation Cadet Program. He was commissioned in the Marine Corps in 1943. Glenn was awarded a bachelor of science in engineering from Muskingum in 1962.

During his World War II service, Glenn flew 59 combat missions in the South Pacific. Following the war, he remained in the military as a Marine pilot and served as an instructor in advanced flight training. During the Korean conflict, he flew 63 missions with Marine Fighter Squadron 311 and 27 missions as an exchange pilot with the Air Force.

He holds the Air Medal with 18 Clusters for his combat service and has been awarded the Distinguished Flying Cross on six occasions. He is the recipient of numerous other honors, including the Congressional Space Medal of Honor.

In 1954, Glenn won an assignment as a Marine test pilot and, in 1957, set a transcontinental speed record for the first flight to average supersonic speeds from Los Angeles to New York. In 1959, he was selected to be one of seven NASA Mercury astronauts from an original pool of 508. Three years later, on February 20, 1962, he made history as the first American to orbit the earth, completing three orbits in a five-hour flight and returning to a hero's welcome.

Glenn retired from the Marine Corps as a colonel in 1965, becoming a business executive with Royal Crown and serving first as a member of the board of directors and then as president of Royal Crown International. During this time, he took an active part in Democratic politics and early environmental protection efforts in Ohio.

In 1974, he was elected to the U.S. Senate, carrying all 88 counties in Ohio. He was reelected in 1980 with the largest margin of votes in Ohio history. Ohioans returned him to the Senate for the third time in 1986, and, in 1992, he again made history by being the first popularly elected senator from Ohio to win four consecutive terms. He retired from the Senate in 1998.

Glenn returned to space from October 29 to November 7, 1998, as a member of NASA's Shuttle STS-95 Discovery mission during which the crew supported 83 research payloads and investigations on space flight and aging. He is the oldest person to have flown in space. During that mission, Glenn made 134 Earth orbits in 213 hours and 44 minutes.

In October 1997, Glenn announced that his papers, documenting his full career, would be archived at The Ohio State University. In September 1998, Ohio State announced the establishment of the John Glenn Institute for Public Service and Public Policy at the university and in July of 2006, the Institute merged with Ohio State's School of Public Policy & Management to form the John Glenn School of Public Affairs.

Glenn has been married to Anna (Annie) Margaret Castor since 1943. They have a son, Dave, and a daughter, Lyn, and two grandchildren.

## Morton H. Halperin—*Member*

Morton H. Halperin is a consultant to the Open Society Institute and the Open Society Policy Center. He is also a Senior Fellow at the Center for American Progress.

Halperin served in the federal government in the Clinton, Nixon, and Johnson administrations and was involved in nuclear policy and arms control issues in all three administrations. From December 1998 to January 2001 he was Director of the Policy Planning Staff at the Department of State. From February 1994 to March 1996, he was a Special Assistant to the President and Senior Director for Democracy at the National Security Council. In 1993, he was a consultant to the Secretary of Defense and the Under Secretary of Defense for Policy and was nominated by the President for the position of Assistant Secretary of Defense for Democracy and Peacekeeping. In 1969, he was a Senior Staff member of the National Security Council staff with responsibility for National Security Planning. From July 1966 to January 1969, he worked in the Department of Defense where he served as Deputy Assistant Secretary of Defense (International Security Affairs), responsible for political-military planning and arms control.

Halperin was a Senior Fellow at the Council on Foreign Relations from January 2001 to June 2003 (directing a project on nuclear policy) and from March 1996 to December 1998. From July 1997 through December 1998, he was Senior Vice President of The Century Foundation/Twentieth Century

Fund. From November 1992 to February 1994, Halperin was a Senior Associate of the Carnegie Endowment for International Peace. In 1974, he directed a project on government secrecy for the Twentieth Century Fund. From September 1969 to December 1973, he was a Senior Fellow in Foreign Policy Studies of the Brookings Institution.

In addition to his involvement in nuclear policy, arms control and other foreign policy issues, Halperin worked for many years for the American Civil Liberties Union (ACLU). He served as Director of the Center for National Security Studies from 1975 to 1992. From 1984 to 1992, he was also the Director of the Washington Office of the ACLU.

From 1960 to 1966, Halperin was associated with Harvard University where he was an Assistant Professor of Government, a Research Associate of the Center for International Affairs and Executive Director of the Harvard-MIT Arms Control Seminar. Halperin has taught as a visiting professor at a number of universities, including Columbia, Harvard, MIT, George Washington, Johns Hopkins, and Yale.

Halperin has authored, coauthored and edited more than a dozen books many of them on issues related to nuclear policy and arms control. These include *Strategy and Arms Control* (1961, with Thomas C. Schelling), *Limited War in the Nuclear Age,* (1963), *China and the Bomb* (1965), *Contemporary Military Strategy* (1967), *Bureaucratic Politics and Foreign Policy* (1974), and *Nuclear Fallacy* (1987). He has also authored monographs on nuclear policy issues for IDA and IISS among others and contributed articles to a number of book collections, newspapers, magazines, and journals, including The New York Times, The Washington Post, The New Republic, Harpers, Foreign Affairs, and Foreign Policy.

Born in Brooklyn, New York in 1938, Halperin received a BA from Columbia College in 1958 and a Ph.D. in International Relations from Yale University in 1961. He is a member of the Council on Foreign Relations and the American Civil Liberties Union.

## Lee H. Hamilton—*Member*

Lee H. Hamilton became president and director of the Woodrow Wilson International Center for Scholars in January 1999. Prior to becoming president and director of the Wilson Center Mr. Hamilton served for thirty-four years as a United States Congressman from Indiana. During his tenure he served as Chairman and Ranking Member of the House Committee on Foreign Affairs (now the Committee on International Relations), and chaired the Subcommittee on Europe and the Middle East from the early 1970s until 1993. Mr. Hamilton also served as chairman of the Permanent Select Committee on Intelligence, and the Select Committee to Investigate Covert Arms

Transactions with Iran. Mr. Hamilton established himself as a leading congressional voice on foreign affairs, with particular interests in promoting democracy and market reform in the former Soviet Union and Eastern Europe, promoting peace and stability in the Middle East, expanding U.S. markets and trade overseas, and overhauling U.S. export and foreign aid policies.

Mr. Hamilton has also been a leading figure on economic policy and congressional organization. As chairman of the Joint Committee on the Organization of Congress and a member of the House Standards of Official Conduct Committee, he was a primary draftsman of several House ethics reforms, and worked to promote the integrity and efficiency of Congress as an institution.

In his home state of Indiana, Mr. Hamilton worked hard to improve education, job training, and infrastructure. He established The Center on Congress at Indiana University, serving as director.

Mr. Hamilton remains an important and active voice on matters of international relations and American national security. He served as a commissioner on the United States Commission on National Security in the 21st Century (the Hart-Rudman Commission), and was co-chair with former senator Howard Baker of the Baker-Hamilton Commission to Investigate Certain Security Issues at Los Alamos. He was named vice-chairman of the National Commission on Terrorist Attacks Upon the United States (the 9/11 Commission), which issued its report in July 2004, then co-chaired with Governor Tom Kean the 9/11 Public Discourse Project. In March 2006 he was named co-chairman of the Iraq Study Group. In February 2007 he was appointed to the National War Powers Commission, a private, bipartisan panel led by former Secretaries of State James A. Baker III and Warren Christopher.

Mr. Hamilton's distinguished service in government has been honored through numerous awards in public service and human rights as well as honorary degrees. He is the author of *A Creative Tension—The Foreign Policy Roles of the President and Congress* (2002) and *How Congress Works and Why You Should Care* (2004), and coauthor of *Without Precedent: The Inside Story of the 9/11 Commission* (2006) and *The Iraq Study Group* Report (2006).

Born in Daytona Beach Florida, Mr. Hamilton's family relocated to Tennessee and then Evansville, Indiana. Mr. Hamilton is a graduate of DePauw University and Indiana University law school, and studied for a year at Goethe University in Germany. A former high school and college basketball star, he has been inducted into the Indiana basketball Hall of Fame. Before his election to Congress, he practiced law in Chicago, Illinois, and Columbus, Indiana.

Lee and his wife, the former Nancy Ann Nelson, have three children: Tracy Lynn Souza, Deborah Hamilton Kremer, and Douglas Nelson Hamilton, and five grandchildren: Christina, Maria, McLouis, and Patricia Souza, and Lina Ying Kremer.

## Fred Charles Iklé—*Member*

Fred C. Iklé is a Distinguished Scholar at the Center for Strategic and International Studies. He is currently engaged in studies about the impact of technology on national security, and on the prospects for democracy. He is a member of the Defense Policy Board, a governor of the Smith Richardson Foundation, a Director of the U.S. Committee for Human Rights in North Korea, and an advisory board member of the American Foreign Policy Council.

Prior to joining CSIS in 1988, Iklé was Undersecretary of Defense for Policy during the first and second Reagan administrations. In 1987, he co-chaired the bipartisan Commission on Integrated Long-Term Strategy, which published *Discriminate Deterrence*. Iklé received the highest civilian award of the Department of Defense, the Distinguished Public Service Medal in 1987, and in 1988 he was awarded the Bronze Palm.

From 1973 to 1977, Iklé served Presidents Nixon and Ford as director of the U.S. Arms Control and Disarmament Agency. From 1977 to 1978, he was chairman of the Republican National Committee's Advisory Council on International Security and, from 1979 to 1980, coordinator of Governor Ronald Reagan's foreign policy advisers.

Iklé served for nine years as a director of the National Endowment for Democracy, and in 1999-2000 served as Commissioner on the National Commission on Terrorism. He was director and chairman of Telos Corporation, and director of the advisory board of Zurich Financial Services. From 1968 to 1972, Iklé was head of the Social Science Department of the RAND Corporation. From 1964 to 1967, he was professor of political science at the Massachusetts Institute of Technology. He held positions with the Center for International Affairs at Harvard University (1962-1963), the RAND Corporation (1954-1961), and the Bureau of Applied Social Research at Columbia University (1950-1953).

Iklé is the author of *The Social Impact of Bomb Destruction* (University of Oklahoma Press, 1958); *How Nations Negotiate* (Harper & Row, 1964; reissued by Praeger, and again by Kraus Reprint, 1976); and *Every War Must End* (Columbia University Press, 1970; reissued with new preface in 1991; second reissue with new preface in 2005); and *Annihilation From Within* (New York: Columbia University Press, 2006). Iklé has published many articles in *Foreign Affairs, Fortune, The National Interest*, and op-eds in leading newspapers.

# Keith B. Payne—*Member*

Keith Payne is President and co-founder of the National Institute for Public Policy, a nonprofit research center located in Fairfax, Virginia. At National Institute, he directs and participates in studies on U.S. strategic policy and force posture issues, arms control, BMD, and Russian foreign policy. Payne also is Head of the Graduate Department of Defense and Strategic Studies, Missouri State University (Washington Campus), and in 2005 was awarded the Vicennial Medal for his twenty-one years of teaching at Georgetown University.

On leave from National Institute in 2002 and 2003, Payne served in the Department of Defense as the Deputy Assistant Secretary of Defense for Forces Policy. He received the Distinguished Public Service Medal from Secretary of Defense Rumsfeld, and the Forces Policy office Payne led received a Joint Meritorious Unit Award. In this position, Payne was the head of U.S. delegation in numerous allied consultations and in "Working Group Two" negotiations on BMD cooperation with the Russian Federation.

Payne is the editor-in-chief of *Comparative Strategy: An International Journal*, Chairman of the Strategic Command's Senior Advisory Group Policy Panel, co-chair of the U.S. Nuclear Strategy Forum, and a member of the State Department's International Security Advisory Board. He has served as a participant or leader of numerous governmental and private studies, including White House studies of U.S.-Russian cooperation, Defense Department studies of missile defense, arms control, and proliferation, and as co-chairman of the Department of Defense's Deterrence Concepts Advisory Group. He also has served as a consultant to the White House Office of Science and Technology Policy, and the Arms Control and Disarmament Agency, and participated in the 1998 "Rumsfeld Study" of missile proliferation.

Payne testifies frequently before Congressional Committees, and has lectured on defense and foreign policy issues at numerous colleges and universities in North America, Europe, and Asia. He is the author or co-author of over 100 published articles and sixteen books and monographs. His most recent book is entitled, *The Great American Gamble: Deterrence Policy and Theory from the Cold War to the Twenty-First Century*.

Payne's articles have appeared in major U.S., European and Japanese professional journals, including, *Foreign Affairs, Foreign Policy, Orbis, Europäische Sicherheit, Policy Review, Strategic Review, Washington Quarterly, Jane's Intelligence Review, Militare Spectator, Air University Review, Comparative Strategy, Air Force Magazine, Issues In Science and Technology, Military Review, Parameters, Harper's, The Wall Street Journal, The Christian Science Monitor*, and *USA Today*.

Payne received an A.B. (honors) in political science from the University of California at Berkeley in 1976, studied in Heidelberg, Germany, and in 1981 received a Ph.D. (with distinction) in international relations from the University of Southern California.

## C. Bruce Tarter—*Member*

C. Bruce Tarter is Director Emeritus of the Lawrence Livermore National Laboratory, University of California and was the eighth director to lead the Laboratory since it was founded in 1952. A theoretical physicist by training and experience, he spent most of his career at the Laboratory. As director, he led the Laboratory in its mission to ensure national security and apply science and technology to the important problems of our time. The Laboratory is a principal contributor to the Department of Energy's programs to maintain the U.S. nuclear weapons stockpile and to reduce the international dangers posed by weapons of mass destruction.

Tarter received a bachelor's degree in physics from the Massachusetts Institute of Technology and a Ph.D. from Cornell University. His career at the Livermore Laboratory began in 1967 as a staff member in the Theoretical Physics Division. His research concentrated on supercomputer calculations of the properties of matter at high temperatures and densities, with applications to nuclear weapons, fusion, energy, and astrophysics. He became head of Theoretical Physics in 1978.

During the 1980s, Tarter became a Laboratory leader in establishing stronger ties with the University of California. He served on a number of institutional committees and task forces, and he helped formulate the Laboratory's strategic direction as a member of the Long-Range Planning Committee. In 1988, he joined the ranks of senior management as associate director for Physics, a position that he expanded to include weapons physics, space technology leading to the Clementine mission to the Moon, and a broadly based program in global climate and other environmental research.

Tarter was selected as director in 1994, after serving briefly as deputy director and acting director. He led the Laboratory through the transition to a post–Cold War nuclear weapons world, helping to set the foundation for current programs in stewardship of the U.S. nuclear stockpile. He also worked to build the programs in nonproliferation and counter-terrorism, and in energy, environment, and bioscience. He served as Director through the first half of 2002, then spent a year and a half as Associate Director at Large until his retirement in early 2004.

In addition to his Laboratory activities, Tarter has served in a number of outside professional capacities. These include a six-year period with the Army Science Board, service as an adjunct professor at the University of California at Davis, and membership on the California Council on Science and Technology, the Laboratory Operations Board (Secretary of Energy Advisory Board), Pacific Council on International Policy, Nuclear Energy Research Advisory Committee, the Council on Foreign Relations, the Defense Science Board, and the Corporation and Board of Directors of the Draper Laboratory.

He is a Fellow of the American Physical Society, the American Association for the Advancement of Science, and the California Council on Science and Technology, and received the Roosevelts Gold Medal Award for Science (1998), NNSA Gold Medal for Distinguished Service (2002), the US Department of Energy Exceptional Public Service Award (2002), and the US Department of Energy Secretary's Gold Award (2004).

## Ellen D. Williams—*Member*

Born in Oshkosh, Wisconsin in 1953, Ellen D. Williams grew up in Livonia, Michigan, received her Bachelor of Science from Michigan State University in 1976 and her Ph.D from California Institute of Technology in 1981. She then joined the University of Maryland Physics Department where she established an experimental program designed to push the limits of understanding electronic materials to the atomic level. With funding from the Department of Defense and National Science Foundation, her group pioneered the application of scanning tunneling microscopy to the quantitative determination and interpretation of structural fluctuations, and now applies this approach to the development of novel electronic materials for nanoelectronics applications. Her work has been presented in over 180 refereed publications and has been recognized by numerous awards, including the NSF Presidential Young Investigator award, 1984-89; Office of Naval Research Young Investigator award, 1986-89; American Physical Society - Maria Goeppert-Mayer Award, 1990; Fellow of the American Physical Society, 1993; Fellow of the American Vacuum Society, 1993; University of Maryland Outstanding Woman of the Year, 1996; E.W. Mueller Award, University of Wisconsin, Milwaukee, 1996; Japan Society for the Promotion of Science Fellow, 1996; University of Maryland Distinguished Faculty Research Fellow, 1996-98; American Physical Society David Adler Lectureship Award, 2001; Materials Research Society Turnbull Lectureship, 2003. She was elected to the American Academy of Arts and Sciences in 2003 and the National Academy of Sciences in 2005.

In 1995, Williams established the NSF-supported Materials Research and Engineering Center at the University of Maryland, which supports collaborative research programs and an extensive program of outreach programs designed to encourage and support pre-college students in pursuing careers in science, technology, engineering and mathematical fields. She continues to serve as director of the center, and is also active in professional service including professional committees, review and advisory panels, and editorial boards, which have included American Physical Society prize selection committees (2008, 1998, 1996), Board of Reviewing Editors for Science Magazine (2003-present), Editorial board for Nano Letters (2001-present) and Annual Review of Condensed Matter Physics (2008-present), External advisory committees (Stanford NSCE 2007, U. Chicago MRSEC 1997-present, Harvard NSEC 2003, Cornell NSEC 2003), APS Policy Committee (2005-7), Materials Research Society meeting chair (1999) and Board of Directors (2006-7), external review committees (DOE-BES Materials Science programs 2008, NCSU Physics 2007, LBL Materials Science Division 2003, Rutgers Physics Dept. 2002), member of the Solid State Sciences Committee of the NAS (2001-4), Co-organizer of the National Nanotechnology Initiative Grand Challenges Workshop on Energy 2004).

In 1993, Williams joined the JASONs, an independent government advisory group, and has worked on technical problems covering a wide range of programs including stockpile stewardship, energy sources, nanotechnology, conventional prompt global strike, human performance and phased-array radar systems. Correlated public service activities have included the National Security Panel of University of California President's Council (2000-2007), NNSA Advisory Committee (2001-2), NRC Committee on Nanotechnology for the Intelligence Community (2003-4), AAAS Nuclear Weapons Complex Assessment Committee (2006-7), NRC Committee on Conventional Prompt Global Strike Capability (2007-8), NRC Board on Army Science and Technology (2007-9).

# R. James Woolsey—*Member*

R. James Woolsey is a Venture Partner with VantagePoint Venture Partners of San Bruno, California.

Woolsey also currently is the Annenberg Distinguished Visiting Fellow at the Hoover Institution at Stanford University; chairs the Strategic Advisory Group of the Washington, D.C. private equity fund, Paladin Capital Group; is a Senior Executive Advisor to the consulting firm Booz Allen Hamilton; and is Of Counsel to the Washington, D.C., office of the Boston-based law firm, Goodwin Procter. In the above capacities he specializes in a range of alternative energy and security issues.

Woolsey previously served in the U.S. Government on five different occasions where he held Presidential appointments in two Republican and two Democratic administrations, most recently (1993-95) as Director of Central Intelligence. From July 2002 to March 2008 Woolsey was a Vice President and officer of Booz Allen Hamilton. He was also previously a partner at the law firm of Shea & Gardner in Washington, D.C., now Goodwin Procter, where he practiced for 22 years in the fields of civil litigation, arbitration, and mediation.

During his 12 years of government service, in addition to heading the CIA and the Intelligence Community, Woolsey was Ambassador to the Negotiation on Conventional Armed Forces in Europe (CFE), Vienna, 1989–1991; Under Secretary of the Navy, 1977–1979; and General Counsel to the U.S. Senate Committee on Armed Services, 1970–1973. He was also appointed by the President to serve on a part-time basis in Geneva, Switzerland, 1983–1986, as Delegate at Large to the U.S.–Soviet Strategic Arms Reduction Talks (START) and Nuclear and Space Arms Talks (NST). As an officer in the U.S. Army, he was an adviser on the U.S. Delegation to the Strategic Arms Limitation Talks (SALT I), Helsinki and Vienna, 1969–1970.

Woolsey serves on a range of government, corporate, and nonprofit advisory boards and chairs several, including that of the Washington firm, ExecutiveAction LLC. He serves on the National Commission on Energy Policy. He is currently Co-Chairman (with former Secretary of State George Shultz) of the Committee on the Present Danger. He is Chairman of the Advisory Boards of the Clean Fuels Foundation and the New Uses Council, and a Trustee of the Center for Strategic & Budgetary Assessments. Previously he was Chairman of the Executive Committee of the Board of Regents of The Smithsonian Institution, and a trustee of Stanford University. He has also been a member of The National Commission on Terrorism, 1999–2000; The Commission to Assess the Ballistic Missile Threat to the U.S. (Rumsfeld Commission), 1998; The President's Commission on Federal Ethics Law Reform, 1989; The President's Blue Ribbon Commission on Defense Management (Packard Commission), 1985–1986; and The President's Commission on Strategic Forces (Scowcroft Commission), 1983.

Woolsey has served in the past as a member of boards of directors of a number of publicly and privately held companies, generally in fields related to technology and security, including Martin Marietta; British Aerospace, Inc.; Fairchild Industries; and Yurie Systems, Inc.

Woolsey was born in Tulsa, Oklahoma, and attended Tulsa public schools, graduating from Tulsa Central High School. He received his B.A. degree from Stanford University (1963, With Great Distinction, Phi Beta Kappa), an M.A. from Oxford University (Rhodes Scholar 1963–1965), and an LL.B from Yale Law School (1968, Managing Editor of the Yale Law Journal).

Woolsey is a frequent contributor of articles to major publications, and from time to time gives public speeches and media interviews on the subjects of foreign affairs, defense, energy, and intelligence. He is married to Suzanne Haley Woolsey and they have three sons, Robert, Daniel, and Benjamin.

# Appendix 9

# Commission Support Staff

Paul D. Hughes
Commission Executive Director

Bruce W. MacDonald
Senior Director

Bradley H. Roberts
Senior Researcher and Lead Writer, Institute for
Defense Analyses

Victor A. Utgoff
Senior Researcher, Institute for Defense Analyses

Taylor A. Bolz
Assistant to the Commission

Brian W. Rose
Assistant to the Commission

Markell Miller
Assistant to the Commission, Institute for Defense Analyses

## Assistants to the Commissioners

| | |
|---|---|
| Deborah C. Gordon | Carol Padgett |
| Liz Kurzeila | June Halstead |
| Mary Jane Veno | Nora Coulter |
| Helen Lawing | Denise Steele |
| Nancy Bonomo | Peter Pry |
| Kingston Reif | Wade Boese |
| Jennifer Knepper | Stephanie Koeshall |
| Alicia Godsberg | |

# U.S. Government Liaison Officers

Dr. John R. Harvey
National Nuclear Security Administration

David J. Stein
Dr. Frank Dellerman
Office of the Secretary of Defense,
Department of Defense

Dr. Kerry M. Kartchner
Brandon Buttrick
International Security Advisory Board,
Department of State

Donald M. Hodge
National Intelligence Council

# Assistants to the Expert Working Groups

Jonathan S. Lachman
National Security Strategy and Policies

Chantell L. Murph
Deterrent Force Structure

Matthew J. Squeri
Nuclear Infrastructure

Lisa Andivahis
Countering Proliferation